SHATTERING OUR ASSUMPTIONS

MIRIAM NEFF
DEBRA KLINGSPORN

SHATTERING
OUR
ASSUMPTIONS

BETHANY HOUSE PUBLISHERS
MINNEAPOLIS, MINNESOTA 55438

Published by Bethany House Publishers
A Ministry of Bethany Fellowship, Inc.
11300 Hampshire Avenue South
Minneapolis, Minnesota 55438
Printed in the United States of America.

Library of Congress Cataloging-in-Publication Data

Neff, Miriam.
    Shattering our assumptions : who is today's Christian woman / Miriam Neff and Debra K. Klingsporn.
      p.   cm.
    Includes bibliographical references.
    ISBN 1–55661–686–4
    1. Women—Religious life. 2. Women (Christian theology) 3. Women in Christianity—United States. 4. Women—United States. I. Klingsporn, Debra. II. Title.
BV4527.N363   1996
248.8'43—dc20

96–45769
CIP

We dedicate this book to our daughters and nieces:

Valerie Lynn Neff,
Tracy Gordon,
Haley Way,
Laura Peters,
Erin Jordon,
Jennifer Shelton,
Julie Shelton,
Jackie Shelton,
Laura Kathryn Klingsporn,
Kari Elizabeth Klingsporn,
and
Kirsten Michelle Holliday.

May they live boldly,
choose wisely,
and never lose touch with their dreams.

Acknowledgments

We wish to express our appreciation to the individuals involved in the design, creation, compilation, analysis, and statistical interpretation of the survey: Kathy Dice at Willow Creek Community Church, and John LaRue and Hope Grant at *Christianity Today*.

We also want to thank several women who patiently talked with us about their lives, their faith, and their experiences and allowed us to incorporate their stories into this book: Linda Rios Brook, Anne Carrier, Kathy Downing, Barb Aslesen, and Nancy Schaefer.

Also special thanks to Mary Whelchel for helping distribute the survey and allowing me to survey women who correspond with her organization, The Christian Working Woman.

Contents

Acknowledgments 7
A Personal Word From Miriam Neff 11
About the Survey 15
About the Authors 17
Introduction 19

Section One
Women in the Workplace

1. Tug-of-War of the Heart 25
2. The Gender Jungle 37
3. The Juggling Game 57

Section Two
Women Away From Work

4. Women and Money: Statistics,
   Stress, and Dollars and Cents 79
5. The Perfect Christian Wife
   (and Other Elusive Dreams) 99
6. Mentoring: Reshaping the Assumptions
   of a Younger Generation 123

Section Three
Women Living a Covenant

7. Linda Rios Brook: Living a Covenant 139
8. Never Forever the Same 157
9. Where We Serve, Where We Pray 167
10. Monday Through Saturday:
    Christian Women Today 183

Section Four
References and Resources

Appendix A: The Neff Report:
    Christian Women in Today's Church and Society 193
Appendix B: Recommended Resources 213

A Personal Word From Miriam Neff

Twenty-five years ago, as a new Christian in graduate school at Northwestern University, I was an ardent reader with a love for research. In the introduction of *Sisters of the Heart* (Thomas Nelson Publishers, 1995), I explained the impact this passion has had on reading my most loved book, the Word. With regrets that I had never been able to study at a Christian institution, I asked God to be my Teacher, my Professor. I simply opened my Bible and spread *Strong's Concordance, Vine's Dictionary,* and the *Treasury of Scriptural Knowledge* about me on my apartment floor. Unknowingly, I was ahead of my time.

As one part of my study, I looked up each word related to gender to see if God meant the instruction for me as a woman. Was I included in the lesson or promise, or was it for someone else? I began the practice of using "woman" in place of "man" and "she" in place of "he" whenever it seemed appropriate as I read the Scripture. I knew nothing of feminism or what churches considered appropriate or politically correct regarding roles. I simply loved God and wanted to know what instructions God intended me to follow as I ran the race of life.

The result was a very personalized, blotchy Bible that I treasure even now as a middle-aged woman. Perhaps the result has also been a woman who sees living as an eager Christian disciple as more important than deciphering what she should not do.

As the number of women increases in our seminaries and more women are studying the original Word, the human filter that has seen God only through male eyes will be forever changed.

For decades women who read the Bible were simply grateful that they were *able* to read. Throughout most of history, women could not read and were not allowed to learn. Spiritual growth was dependent on the teaching of others. When the King James Version made Scripture widely available, happily we read:

> Be not thou afraid when one is made rich, when the glory of his house is increased; For when he dieth he shall carry nothing away: his glory shall not descend after him. Though while he lived he blessed his soul: and men will praise thee, when thou doest well to thyself. He shall go to the generation of his fathers; they shall never see light. Man that is in honour, and understandeth not, is like the beasts that perish.
>
> Psalm 49:16–20, KJV

Now research has brought greater clarity to the original text, discovering the word "man" is "mankind" or "humankind" and applies as fully to "woman" as it does to "man." While this might seem insignificant, let me illustrate how much more personal and powerful the text can be when read with more gender-inclusive language:

> Do not be overawed when a woman grows rich,
> when the splendor of her house increases;
> for she will take nothing with her when she dies,
> her splendor will not descend with her.
> Though while she lived she counted herself blessed
> and women praise you when you prosper—
> she will join the generation of her mothers,
> who will never see the light of life.

> A woman who has riches without understanding
> is like the beasts that perish.
>
> Psalm 49:16–20,
>
> with female nouns/pronouns

Because we are writing *for* women and *about* women, my coauthor and I have chosen to use feminine pronouns for the people of God throughout *Shattering Our Assumptions* when quoting from Scripture. Because we recognize that gender-accurate language (sometimes called inclusive language) continues to be a sensitive subject in many churches, we do not wish to offend, nor do we wish to engage in theological debate. We simply feel that as our challenges as Christian women grow, so does our hunger for God. Use of gender-accurate language is a powerful study tool, and one through which God is meeting us, as He has every person who ever sought Him.

This combined love of reading and research opened a new door in my writing. I decided to conduct my own research. As you will soon see, that resulted in going beyond the heavy, blotchy research books that are still strewn on my floor, to composing questions, then a survey. Next came finding women willing to answer questions, then analyzing the results. Each survey page is more than paper and ink. A woman's life is behind every checked box on the survey forms: a woman who loves God, who struggles with living her first love, and who is willing to share that with you.

—Miriam Neff

The Neff Report: About the Survey

This book began as a rather simple research project. In conversations with Kathy Dice, the director of Women's Ministries at Willow Creek Community Church in South Barrington, Illinois, we conceived the idea for a survey of Christian women. We talked of information she would like to know about the women her church serves, to help her staff effectively meet the needs of Christian women.

In selecting groups to approach, I chose churches from coast to coast to get a general geographic sampling. I chose racially diverse churches, as well as a mix of evangelical and charismatic churches. The survey was offered to women in those churches and taken by those who volunteered to do so. In addition to churches, I have surveyed a portion of the women who correspond with The Christian Working Woman, a diverse group geographically and in church representation.

Shattering Our Assumptions also draws from research conducted by Christianity Today, Inc., surveying readers of *Today's Christian Woman*, a magazine with a readership demographic of women ages 35–55 who are active in evangelical churches. Ultimately, I contacted ten churches and received 1,200 completed surveys; however, the statistical compilation and analysis is based on 1,000 surveys received prior to the compilation deadline. Although the 200 surveys received after the compilation and analysis were used for reference purposes, they are not tabulated in the statistical results.

Finally, although the survey did include questions related to Christian women's sexuality, we concluded that dealing with sexuality issues was beyond the scope of this book.

About the Authors

Miriam Neff and Debra Klingsporn have much in common. Both are writers, professionals, wives, and mothers. Both are committed Christian women active in their churches and communities. And both are in positions affording them an opportunity to observe women today—but from radically different vantage points.

Miriam is a counselor in a large urban high school in the Chicago metro area. In that role, she sees the young women of tomorrow, a generation removed from the radical feminism of bra-burnings and strident rhetoric. Despite their exposure to women's rights advocates and working moms, these girls aren't necessarily looking at educational goals and career options; all too often their most pressing concerns are (1) how to get the good-looking guys and/or (2) whether or not they're pregnant. Miriam's goal is to challenge these teenage girls to think beyond the constraining refrains of pop songs playing in their minds, beyond their hormones, and beyond their present circumstances.

Miriam is an author, host of a national radio broadcast, and frequent speaker at women's conferences and retreats. Throughout the year, she talks with literally hundreds of women across the country. She juggles a multidimensional career, a long-term marriage, and the mothering responsibilities that go along with raising four children—and she has weathered the turbulence of parenting teenagers.

Debra Klingsporn is a professional writer with fifteen years experience in the publishing industry. Prior to her work as an independent writer and marketing communications consultant, she was vice president of a public relations firm based in Chicago. Before joining the public relations firm, she was the director of marketing for one of the largest Christian publishing companies. Married to a senior staff minister in a large suburban church and the mother of two young daughters, she works out of a home office, ever wrestling with the blurred boundaries of being a work-at-home mom. She has spoken to women's groups, couples' classes, and singles' study groups. Although her life bears the stereotypical trademarks—married to a minister, suburban home, Brownie troop leader (and yes, she even drives a minivan)—she chafes at being too readily pigeonholed within the trappings of traditionalism.

In *Shattering Our Assumptions* the authors have written both independently of each other and worked collaboratively. Due to the personal nature of their writing in some sections of *Shattering Our Assumptions*, the authors are identified when writing in the first person.

Introduction

When the words "Christian" and "women" are thrown together, stereotypes and assumptions quickly come to mind— whether we like it or not. Words become labels. Labels convey values. And values determine our choices.

Think about it. All we have to do is toss out a few well-worn words and the stereotypes and assumptions start piling up: "submissive" versus "feminist," "assertive" versus "demure," "career" versus "motherhood." Add "change" to the mix and suddenly the discussion moves into fast forward.

Shattering Our Assumptions began as a survey designed to find out about the multifaceted dimensions of our lives as Christian women. What we learned through the process shattered a few of *our* assumptions.

We looked at the lives of hundreds of Christian women and listened to the stories of many individuals. Drawing upon the survey results, we also looked at general census statistics, Gallup polls, research projects, interviews, and other information sources. What we found has been surprising, refreshing, sobering, challenging, and intriguing—just what we hope this book will be for our readers. When it comes to the reality of Christian women's lives at work, at home, and at church, we are convinced that many of us shatter more than a few stereotypes.

As authors, we came to this project interested in the confusion and consequences of the rapidly changing roles for
women in our world. As women, we feel the incredible ambi-
guity and stress of change; our personal journeys have been
marked by changing roles, changing circumstances, changing
perspectives. We initially wanted to write a book about change,
how dramatically it affects every aspect of our lives as Christian
women, and what God is saying to us through the changes.

As the project developed, we realized addressing issues of
change quickly taps into issues of relationships, roles, careers,
and longings. Our lives as Christian women defy easy catego-
rizations—we work, we pray, we parent, we love, we serve. One
leads to the other, overlaps the other, intersects with the other,
and before you know it, categories are blurred, roles are inter-
twined, and labels become simplistic.

We also came to this project realizing that for Christian
women the stakes are higher. Not only do we as women juggle
multiple roles, cultural changes, and conflicting demands—as
Christians we hope to make a difference in our world. We desire
to do justice, love mercy, and walk humbly with our God (Micah
6:8) somewhere between getting the grocery shopping done,
folding the laundry, and hopefully putting it away before the
clothes are worn again (Debra's goal—Miriam relinquished this
goal with the arrival of child number four!).

Although we consider our combined experiences valuable,
we recognize that our life and faith can't possibly tell the whole
story of what's happening in other women's lives. We've both
read books based on the writer's experience which wasn't true
to *our* experience, and found ourselves responding with a silent,
"So what?"

Or worse, we've read books that have arrived at conclusions
that were unrealistic and unworkable for our situations. Miriam
once tried to organize her daily schedule by a Christian author's
system of time management, complete with notebook, calendar,

and lists. While it worked for some of her friends, her attempt resulted in disaster. She had too many children, too little money, and spiritual gifts that didn't fit the formula. Debra read a book advocating prayerful weight management—and gained ten pounds. What works for one may not work for all.

So why write a book, or more importantly, why take precious time and energy to *read* a book dealing with the significant changes confronting Christian women today? The answer is simple: *We need perspective.* Hearing the reality in other women's lives becomes a valuable mirror to our lives; and when our experiences as women are completely different, hearing from others opens windows that give us new views of our own world.

Shattering Our Assumptions, a book based on a survey of 1,200 Christian women, provides that perspective. This book was designed to find out about women's lives at work, at home, at church, and in the broader cultural context. We asked Christian women what's important and what's marginal. Based on our research, *Shattering Our Assumptions* looks at what causes us stress, what brings satisfaction, and what we can do differently in each of the three major arenas of our lives: work, home and family, and our faith.

The first section looks at factors affecting workplace stress and our unique perspective as Christian women. The second section looks at women and money, marriage, and mentoring. Although we deal briefly with the ideologies and cultural influences that impact our lives as women, we recognize that entire *books* are written addressing the issues of feminism, stereotypes, and cultural influences. Our intention in this section is not to be clinically thorough, but, rather, pragmatically informative. We've written this section as a practical tool to help determine what's right for us as we make choices and deal with changes— as Christians, as women, as individuals.

The third section looks at what is truly the most important: our faith. What difference does our spirituality make in the twenty-four-hour-a-day/seven-day-a-week reality of our lives? Although we are active in church, for many of us, the sources for spiritual growth and deepening our faith are found through other avenues. What are those avenues? If we don't feel supported at church, how and where do we go to grow in our walk with Christ? And how do we manage to carve out the time for solitude and study? These are significant questions. These are significant issues for most women. The final section offers what we hope is a uniquely feminine approach to balancing the active life of the church member with the reflective seeker in each of us.

Miriam surveyed 1,200 Christian women to better see the big picture. Debra interviewed numerous women to see how they lived their faith. While research and statistics can tell us what's happening in the big picture, there *is* no big picture but for the combined brush strokes of each inch of canvas. The impact of 1,200 Christian women is the collective influence of one woman, and another, and another, individually making daily decisions and choices reflecting their commitment to Christ. Our world has changed. Our society has changed. Our church has changed. God has not. God's presence in the lives of Christian women today testifies to an unchanging covenant of grace and the resilient creativity and courage of the feminine spirit.

By the grace of this unchanging God we serve, we came together on this project to look at the realities of women's lives. As we complete the writing of this book, our prayer is that *Shattering Our Assumptions* will offer encouragement to women feeling fragmented by multiple demands, free women from stereotypes which no longer do justice to Christian women, and, hopefully, shatter a few assumptions surrounding our theological understanding of who and what we are called to be.

> Grace and peace,
> Miriam Neff and
> Debra Klingsporn

Section One

Women in the Workplace

After God created male and female, He made a precious pronouncement. He affirmed that His work was good. Diverse and good, intended for teamwork not competition, intended to enhance not to destroy. No matter what the arena, the idea of different sexes was a good one.

"Finally, sisters, stay focused. If it's true, noble, if it's right, pure, lovely, if it's admirable, if it's excellent, keep it in center focus. The God of peace will be with you."

Philippians 4:8–9, author's paraphrase

One

Tug-of-War of the Heart

M iriam speaks:

"My tummy hurts, Mom."

My seven-year-old son looks at me with pleading eyes, that look every mother recognizes.

Uh-oh. Now what do I do? I'm new on my job, trying my best to do well and make a good impression. I can't stay home from work. My child-care alternatives don't include sick kids. My options are few.

I tuck my business card in his pocket.

"If it hurts bad, ask the school nurse to call me at this number."

I watch him walk slowly down the sidewalk, his little backpack sagging.

The tug-of-war in my heart is painful. The image of his slow steps down the sidewalk replay through my mind every mile as I drive to work accompanied by worry, guilt, and doubts about the choices I've made and the parenting memories I am creating. With each phone call that day, I wonder if I will hear the words,

"Miriam, this is Donna James, the school nurse. Your son is in my office with a fever of 101. When can you pick him up?"

The coffee cup sits undisturbed on the table in front of us, the steam rising in vapors like the unspoken words between us.

My friend has decided to go back to work. The decision was a difficult tug-of-war between financial realities and her desire to be with her children full-time. She and her husband talked long and hard, looked at the options, and concluded that her employment was the best alternative at the time. As we sit together at a holiday gathering, she tearfully watches her two preschoolers with a sense of impending loss, knowing that in a few weeks she will have fewer moments to watch their puppylike, rough-and-tumble play. From the kitchen she overhears her mother, unaware of the impending change, say to her aunt, "I don't want anyone else raising my grandchildren!"

"Miriam, I need my mom's support, not her disapproval."

Debra speaks:

This was the day of the class party, the first party of the year. The older kids planned the games, activities, and treats for the younger grades—and she was one of the "older kids" now. She had taken her party-planning job seriously, remembering to shop for the party supplies, blowing up balloons all evening and early in the morning before school, designing and creating her own costume. She was quite proud of herself—and she couldn't wait for her mother to see what she and her classmates had put together.

Since kindergarten she had wanted her mom to be one of the room moms, but with her mother's work schedule, it wasn't possible. This year was different. This year her mom agreed to be a room mom. She would be at the party. Her mom would see what a great job she'd done.

Then came the lengthy phone call the night before the party, followed by a few other phone calls. As soon as she overheard her mother's words, she stopped blowing up balloons and sat quietly in the big rocking chair.

"Karen, I'm really behind the eight ball on this project. Can you fill in for me at the class party? I can drop off the cups and plates in the morning, but I really need some uninterrupted work time."

Disappointment was plainly visible on her face. She knew without asking—her mother wouldn't be there.

She was old enough to understand the explanation, but the words didn't ease her disappointment. Debra knew—because Debra is her mom.

Miriam speaks:

I sat in my office, fingers drumming on the top of my desk, staring at my calendar. I knew I was allowing myself a pity party. Although I love my job as a high school counselor, on that day I didn't want to be at my desk. I wanted to be in Florida with my husband at a gathering of national Christian leaders fasting for the spiritual welfare of our country.

When we received the invitation from Bill and Vonette Bright, my husband and I were thrilled. As a Christian educator and parent, I have seen prayer and fasting move the unmovable, change the unchangeable, and beat the unbeatable odds. I wanted to GO. I wanted to be there, experiencing the community of those Bill and Vonette Bright would bring together. But as soon as I looked at the dates on the invitation, I knew I couldn't go. I had to be at work.

On the first day of the fast I sat in my office repeatedly glancing at my calendar with a sense of disappointment. While I could fast, I could not share the sense of community in prayer. I was missing a great beginning. Next to my calendar, a grinning six-month-old baby smiled at me from a photograph, eyes crinkling with glee. The words written on the back of the photo-

graph flashed through my mind, "Ms. Neff, I wouldn't be here
if it wasn't for you." The words, written as if the baby were
speaking directly to me, were the way one of my sixteen-year-
old students had thanked me for a conversation we'd had when
she first realized she was pregnant.

Many months earlier, the young mother-to-be had come to
see me when she thought she had only one choice: abortion. We
talked at length and I encouraged her to consider other options.
The teenager had chosen life—and a photograph of a beautiful
six-month-old baby boy reminded me of the reason I was missing out on a prayer and fasting conference. Yes, I was at work,
not praying and fasting in community where part of my heart
longed to be. But I was at work—where I belonged.

More months have passed. Today a wedding invitation sits
on my desk inviting me to the wedding of this toddler's parents.
How can I entertain myself at a pity party, mourning all I've
missed because I'm at work? I have no regrets. The pity party
ends; the tug-of-war continues.

WOMEN AND OUR WORK

The tug-of-war of the heart for women is real. Juggling priorities. Making choices. Trying to wear too many hats, fulfill too
many roles. We are wives, moms, Christians—and the majority
of us work in some capacity outside the home. Whether we work
in a full-time career, a part-time vocation, choose not to work
for a period of time, or choose to return to work after a time
away, work is the source of both great satisfaction—and incredible stress. While women working in the marketplace is one of
the most rapidly changing forces in our society today, it is also
at the center point of inner struggle for many Christian women.

My research and a survey conducted by *Today's Christian
Woman* reflect that two-thirds of the women polled work outside their homes. Over half with children under eighteen work
outside their homes. Over half of the moms with newborns

reenter the employed-outside-home category within one year. In other words, Christian women are working outside their homes in greater numbers than the general population!

Our agenda is not to debate whether one choice is better than the other, whether women making one choice are acting in a more godly manner than the other. Rather, our agenda is to reflect the reality of women's experience. By holding a mirror to our lives and reflecting the experience and perspective of 1,000 Christian women, we can examine whether our life choices correspond to our life goals, whether the theological influences in our lives are enhancing or hindering our priorities, and how we can create a better balance in the ongoing tug-of-war of the heart.

Before looking in that mirror, however, let's first ask, "Why?" Why do we put ourselves under so much stress? Working never simplifies our lives, and our choices are rarely easy: deciding if a child is *really* sick (too sick to go to school or simply wanting to stay home that day), listening to a friend struggle with the question of what choice is best for her, disappointing a child when memory making and job responsibilities collide. Conflicting demands between home and work are daily reality for women today.

Why *do* we live the tug-of-war of the heart?

Are the reasons purely financial? Are we stressing out our lives because of the money? Assuming women work for survival, or that we work primarily to pay our bills, is a natural assumption. But it simply isn't so.

Starting with statistics, how much money do women earn? In 1991 the average income of a nation's household was $29,943. Women earned seventy-one cents to every dollar earned by men. Among men and women with more than twelve years of school completed, men earned $700 weekly while women earned $400. Among men and women with less than twelve years of school, men earned $350 weekly and women earned $200.

Probably the most dramatic difference in income is between married-couple families and female-headed families. The average income per married-couple family was $41,260. Households headed by a woman with children earned $13,092.[1]

I remember a cry of alarm in the early 1980s that women entering the marketplace in significant numbers was greed personified. Critics of women working outside the home assumed that women were taking jobs away from men only to take their paychecks straight to the local mall for frivolous shopping. As any working woman knows, nothing could be further from the truth.

Many high-profile Christian leaders continue to advocate a theological perspective that limits a woman's "calling" to that of motherhood. The message we hear from many churches and Christian media perpetuates the myth: Christian women who work only do so to pay the bills; women who are *really* committed to Christ would prefer to be home with their kids.

Although this perspective may be true for some Christian women, it certainly isn't true for a significant percentage of Christian women.

The facts speak for themselves. If we create a pie of the 68 percent of the women who are working, we could carve it into thirds. One-third are single women and single mothers, heads of households who put bread on the table and a roof overhead. Another third are married; their income plus that of their spouse equals an income of poverty level or below. In other words, their husbands may be students, unemployed, disabled, or they both work at low-income jobs. The other third are women such as Debra and I who work for a host of reasons other than survival. We work because we want to; it is our choice, and more importantly—it is our calling.

In my survey of 1,000 Christian women, the percentage of working women was *higher* than the national statistics; 73 percent of the Christian women surveyed were employed, but the pie in our research was similar to general statistics. Most Christian working women do so with less financial compensation than their male counterparts.

If money is the primary reason we work, the facts suggest the financial compensation isn't worth the stress created. There has to be more to this tug-of-war of the heart—and there is.

Although every woman has her own reasons, our research reflected a significant common denominator in Christian women's reasons for working—and surprisingly *money was not the primary motivation.*

In my survey, I asked the women to rank in order of priority the rewards of their choice to work outside their home. The results? "Fulfilling their calling" was the number one reward cited by working Christian women. Receiving a paycheck was secondary.

These responses are more than cold statistics. Christian women view work as more than a job. We view our work as *fulfilling a calling,* and gain far more than simple dollars and cents. Work meets a deep hunger for serving the Lord, for making a significant contribution to families and communities, and work brings us deep satisfaction. Nonetheless, our work is also the source of significant stress. What a paradox! Yet the paradox of fulfillment and stress coming from the same source is one that rings true for every woman. We experience that paradox in our personal relationships, our families, and in our workplaces. The tug-of-war of the heart is a reality for every woman.

Women live in the crossfire of multiple demands, conflicting priorities, and ever-changing roles and circumstances. How we make our choices and determine our priorities, how we respond to the impact of roles, stereotypes, and expectations, and how we determine our response to God's call are significant questions for any woman.

We live in a society of mixed messages and conflicting values. If an alien from outer space landed on earth and tried to figure out what matters to women by reading newspapers, listening to radio, and watching television, the alien's impressions could easily be skewed. The conclusion might be that the biggest issue for women of faith is abortion, followed by losing weight via Jenny Craig.

The alien would meet

- Nike, who tells us to "Just do it!" (Do what? Work out? Ahhh, if intentions could make it so!);
- McDonald's (the all-American diet staple, which then leads us back to our friend Jenny!); and
- Reebok, who tells the alien there's an athlete in every woman—and we daily run the triathlon of keeping the dishes done (usually), paying the bills on time (well, on time *most* of the time), monitoring (at least minimally) kids' homework, and *sigh* the list could go on.

For Christian women trying to live out their faith, the list is even more demanding, the expectations even greater. At Miriam's stage of life, she invests emotional energy and countless hours living her faith when she visits an overcrowded apartment to deliver homework to a suspended student, or when she drives to a funeral home to hug a young husband—a former student whose wife has just taken her life. She goes home to her teen and young adult children to exercise the faith of letting go at the same time as continually sending the message, "I'll always be your mom, but I won't wash the pizza pan or pay your charge card bill."

For women in other stages of life, the issues may be different, but the challenges are no less demanding. Every mom knows the craziness of frantic schedules: shuttling kids to lessons, doctors' appointments, school functions, and activities, all the while trying to maintain some sense of self in the shuffle. We've all heard divorced women struggle with the rebuilding of their lives: the financial adjustments, the emotional turmoil, the pain of starting over. And many of us have watched young women pursue college degrees, begin careers, marry and have kids, and postpone career goals and aspirations for the all-consuming challenge of full-time mothering. Single women struggle with perceptions that they can be on *all* committees because they have so much spare time and that they are continually man-shopping. Many enjoy some solitude, and the survey shows high personal satisfaction.

In short, the alien would miss the substance of what matters most to women, what our *real* daily struggles are.

Nearly two thousand years ago, the apostle Paul wrote timeless words in Hebrews 12 about running the race—and women have been running, huffing and puffing, ever since. The unexpected surprises us. The changes at times overwhelm us. The mixed messages confuse us. Running the race can be difficult.

As the authors of this book, we have come together from different backgrounds, different circumstances, and different life stages, to address the how's and why's of the issues surrounding changes, priorities, roles, and stereotypes. We have seen Christian women, both young and old, struggle with limitations, often imposed by church teachings and religious stereotypes, rather than experiencing the freedom to explore, grow, and change—a freedom grounded in balanced biblical teaching.

Miriam's research and Debra's interviews show that while we expect to run the race bonded with "women-folk" unity, in reality, often we sense competition. Moms at home strive to prove their choice was right. Employed moms run for survival. Christian women who have chosen not to have children or cannot have children are simultaneously envied and excluded. Unmarried women think married women enjoy companionship, while, in fact, many are lonely. Single women are more satisfied than many assume.

Furthermore, Miriam's research found that

- two of the three most significant sources of stress in Christian women's lives are also two sources of greatest fulfillment: work and family.

- Christian women *are* working—and not just to make ends meet. With 73 percent of our respondents employed, a higher percentage of Christian women are working than the general national average. Even more surprising than the percentage of Christian women working is the primary reason or reward for their continued employment. When asked to rank the rewards of their employment, the number one reward was "fulfilling my spiritual calling."
- As women, we wrestle with the compartmentalization of the workplace, family responsibilities, and church life. We juggle the demands of career, continuing to be responsible for most child and home care, while we seek to serve our churches in ways which effectively use our gifts. Women are often left feeling like ringmasters in a three-ring circus rather than whole persons.
- Although more than half the women surveyed (52 percent) believe the Bible teaches that women can hold leadership positions in the church, our beliefs are at odds with our experience. Women with leadership skills are twice as likely to serve in leadership positions in organizations *outside* of their church than in their church.
- Although Christian women feel their relationship to God is very important, our research and interviews reveal that women frequently don't feel supported by their church. The emphasis in many churches on "family values" isn't necessarily supported by "family-friendly" policies. Many women believe a significant gap exists between these two.

The dilemmas Debra and I faced—a sick child and no backup child care, a conflict between a daughter's hopes and a mother's responsibilities, and the inner turmoil of making difficult choices—were readily resolved. My son was fine once he got to school. Debra made it to her daughter's class party *and* made much-needed progress on her project. And a three-by-five snapshot of a six-month-old baby provided the reminder I needed to regain my perspective. Other workplace challenges are not so easily resolved.

My survey and Debra's interviews indicate that Christian working women need and want training for furthering their careers. We want help with the demands of our jobs. We want and need encouragement in our work, our family life, and our churches. We need support in juggling all we do. And we want to enable ourselves to handle the demands that pull us to extremes where work crowds out balanced living.

Who we are privately, professionally, spiritually—at various life stages—is an ongoing issue for women today, because it taps into the deeper question confronting every woman who's made a serious commitment to Christ: "Who am I and what is God calling me to? Do the answers to those questions change with the changing stages of my life?"

The issues of career, marriage, family, personal growth, and spiritual commitment are profound for women today. As we reflect on these issues and their impact on our lives, we hope *Shattering Our Assumptions* will encourage you to listen to your dreams and free you from artificially imposed limitations. We hope to offer you multiple options rather than either/or's. We've tried to address the confusion of too many ought to's and offer clarity for women wrestling with conflicting priorities.

As Christian women, no matter in what stage of life we find ourselves, we face the realities of gender issues, juggling priorities, and knowing when to compromise and when to stand firm. We hope to challenge your thinking, perhaps shatter a few of *your* assumptions, and in so doing enable you to decrease the stress, increase the joy, and balance the tension in the ongoing tug-of-war of the heart.

NOTE

1. Sam Roberts, *Who We Are* (New York: Time Books, 1993), p. 166.

Two

The Gender Jungle

ebra speaks:

D   I stood facing the window, airport noise in the background, with tears rolling down my cheeks. I no longer bothered to wipe away the tears. I let them roll, blinking into the blurred vision, seeing nothing, wishing I were already home.

I had blown it. Blown it big time. My mind was numb, my stomach was churning, and I couldn't get on that plane fast enough.

I'd cried, prayed, called my husband, prayed some more. As I stood in the airport, leaning against the terminal window, nothing I did could stop the constant mental replay of the morning's events. I simply let the tears come.

I had flown in for a meeting, a meeting I thought was going to be a simple face-to-face with an author to go over a marketing plan. The meeting was scheduled by my supervisor, head of the publishing division of a large Christian communications company. He had read over the marketing plan, approved it, and arranged with the author to get together to go over it.

I was always a little nervous going into a marketing meeting with authors—kind of like going to the dentist. For the most part, you know what to expect, but there's always the possibility of an unanticipated development. But I had presented countless marketing plans. Pre-meeting jitters were normal and I was prepared. The plan had been revised and improved numerous times; I knew it backward and forward; I'd anticipated the author's questions and concerns and knew what we as the publisher could do to address those concerns. I was ready—or so I thought.

When my supervisor and I arrived at the author's office, we were greeted warmly and shown into the large, formal boardroom. Masculine leather chairs surrounded a long, imposing conference table in the wood-paneled chambers. As we waited, one by one we were joined by the author's associates. As the first few gentlemen joined us, I thought nothing of it. We exchanged greetings, made small talk, joked about the weather. As the group continued to expand, I began to feel uncomfortable. For one thing, I'd only brought four copies of the marketing plan: one for the author, one for my boss (the publisher), my copy, and an extra. But by the time the author joined us, nearly a half dozen men lined either side of the conference table. As the only woman present, I felt outnumbered and conspicuous.

We quickly asked to have additional copies of the plan made and the meeting got underway. By that time, I knew all was not well. This meeting wasn't a marketing plan presentation—this was a Christian corporate firing squad and I was the target. The questions started coming at me. One by one, they drew their sights, took aim, and fired. By the end of the two-hour meeting, my marketing career was hemorrhaging and the marketing plan was full of holes.

"Flight 496 is now boarding passengers seated in rows 15–22. Please have your boarding pass ready."

The anonymous voice on the loudspeaker interrupted my

mental replays. I was jarred back to the present task. Getting home.

I needed no reminder. My boarding pass was in my hand and I was ready. I wanted to be home, home where my husband could remind me that I still had a life.

On the flight home, as the embarrassment and humiliation subsided, I began the process of a mental meeting post mortem. How could the meeting have gone so badly? Why did I not know we were to meet with an entire staff? My boss knew the plan, knew we were not going out with a marketing "dog-and-pony" show, yet he did nothing to redirect the firing squad as the author's expectation of a full-blown, knock-their-socks-off multimedia presentation became apparent. I felt like a fool—and, in retrospect, I was naive.

The author with whom we were meeting was the single largest revenue-producing author for our publishing company. (That alone would have justified a full-blown, knock-their-socks-off multimedia presentation; I've never made the mistake of an "undersell" since.) A well-known national advocate of family values, he had long championed the perspective that a Christian woman's place was in the home. I was young, ambitious, bright—and not only was I not "in the home," I was the only woman in a highly visible executive position on the staff of a large Christian publishing company. We were coming to that meeting with significantly different theological perspectives on who should even *be* at that meeting. I was definitely not in the "right" place at the right time.

I was under the impression that we were having a one-on-one meeting to solidify a marketing plan, answer questions, and make final adjustments based on the author's input. I'm not sure what the author had been told prior to the meeting or why he clearly expected a different kind of presentation. But as the clash of expectations became apparent, so too did the clash of appropriate gender roles. I was the only woman in a boardroom of

men, each of whom was married to a "stay-at-home" wife. This
demographic homogeneity was not happenstance. In their corporate culture, God had ordained a right and proper order for
males and females—men lead, women follow—and I was completely out of sync with those clearly defined roles. I was not a
secretary making photocopies or an administrative assistant or-
ganizing complex arrangements. I was a director of marketing,
the strategic thinker behind a plan affecting millions of dollars
in long-term revenue. If the players in that boardroom were the
black and white pieces in a chess match, I was a red checker
someone had mistakenly thrown on the board—a piece that
didn't fit in the game.

I am quite sure there was no malice intended at that imposing conference table that day. There was no intentional effort
to shoot down a marketing plan presented by a woman. No one
was "out to get me." In fact, the gender undercurrents were exactly that—silent, invisible undertows that pulled the meeting
into a deep black whirlpool of ineffective communication. I had
been caught in the crossfire of quickly changing women's roles,
slow-to-change corporate cultures, and deeply held religious biases. What became painfully apparent to me was the degree to
which roles and expectations were at odds, and the result was a
disastrous meeting.

*"The captain has turned on the fasten seat belts light. In prep-
aration for our arrival, please put your seat backs in their upright
position, store your tray tables, and be sure your seat belt is fas-
tened. We will be arriving in approximately fifteen minutes."*

By the time my flight landed, I had regained some degree of
self-confidence and my mind raced with "damage-control" pos-
sibilities. One simple idea became the damage-control action
plan.

"Kip, I don't need to tell you that we've got a problem," I
said as I walked into the publisher's office Monday morning,
"but I think I've got a solution.

"We've worked with this author for a long time and we've never had something like this happen. Think about it. What's different in the author/publisher relationship is me. Every other project has had a man as the primary project manager. I've been involved in developing and executing the previous marketing plans, but in a support role, not as the front person. So, here's my idea.

"The plan is good; you and I both know that. What if we revise it slightly, just enough to warrant another meeting with George.[1] Then, instead of having me present the plan, what if we make a big deal about hiring an outside consultant to be a project manager, someone well-known in the industry with proven experience—and someone that's a man. We fly him out to meet with George to make the presentation. I still do the work, but it gets me out of the author relations loop and puts the focus back on our performance as a company. At this point, we've got a lot to gain and little to lose."

The man I proposed as the project manager was almost an icon in the industry. He'd been in publishing thirty years, had an impeccable reputation for marketing savvy, and he was the individual who had first hired me nearly seven years earlier. We worked well together and respected each other.

"You know, Deb, that's not a bad idea," Kip said thoughtfully. "That could work. Let me think it over."

The outcome? The damage-control plan went into effect. I made minor revisions in the plan. The colleague I'd proposed became the project manager. He met with the author, presented the plan, and came back with reports of a satisfied author and an approved marketing plan. Damage control complete.

GENDER ISSUES IN THE WORKPLACE

That day in the airport was more than ten years ago, and I still feel a certain incredulity that essentially the same marketing plan was presented twice to the same author, and the factor that made the difference was primarily one of gender. To this day, I'm sure the author would deny it, if he even *remembered* it. But I remember, vividly, the devastating feelings of failure, the painful feelings of inadequacy, the profound feelings of self-doubt and confusion following that meeting.

Gender issues in the workplace are real—and the Christian community is not immune. If anything, Christian women are at greater risk of remaining trapped within prescribed roles, or struggling with the same mixed messages I have, precisely *because* of pervasive religious teaching and thinking. Employment within a Christian institution may increase negative gender discrimination rather than reduce it.

In my early twenties, I was an eager student of popular Christian writers, teachers, and leaders who upheld traditional biblical interpretations concerning the roles of men and women. I read their works unquestioningly. The man is the head of the household. (Ephesians 5:23 exclusively. No Ephesians 5:21 or explanations of what that verse means by commanding *all* of us to submit to one another.) The woman is to submit to his leadership. (No research on the definition of "submit" in the original language.) I sat in countless college Bible study groups, studying Proverbs 31 verse by verse, always through the theological lens of our "God-ordained" role as "submissive women." But then I graduated, and wasn't married. Well, how do you let a man be the head of a house when there's no man *in* the house? I even remember asking in one of the studies, "What if you never marry?" The question was not welcomed, nor did I ever get a satisfactory answer.

I started working as a reporter for a daily newspaper, still waiting to fulfill my "proper" role as a godly woman—and still there was no man on the scene. By the time I met my husband, I was "upwardly mobile" in a publishing career. I did my job well, learned fast, and got results; I kept getting promoted, gaining more responsibility, moving into positions of increasing authority. Fortunately, I married a man much more open-minded about God's view of women's roles than I was. Rather than forcing my identity into a narrowly defined formula, i.e., "submissive wife, godly woman," he encouraged me, supported me, and challenged my theological thinking. When a promotion was offered which would involve significant business travel and more time away from home (and him), his response was simply, "Honey, I know you can *do* this job. Do you *want* this job?" Little did I know I had married a budding feminist.

Like a butterfly emerging from its safe but restrictive cocoon, astonished to discover that it has wings to fly, my professional success came as a complete surprise to me. I never intended to compete in a man's world, defy tradition, or reverse roles. I simply kept doing what I was good at; I kept doing the next thing God put before me, all the while yearning to be a godly Christian woman.

Based on what my understanding of a "godly Christian woman" was at that time, I usually came up short in my self-evaluations. I was never good at being submissive ("submissive" being defined in the '70s and '80s conservative Christian culture as relatively voiceless and voteless in the marriage relationship or body of believers.) I had to *work* at learning when to listen— and when to keep my mouth shut. Leadership and organizational skills came as naturally to me as breathing. I could run a meeting and keep the agenda moving, develop a strategic plan and keep it on budget, or take on a project and get results. Yet for years, every time I read a book about the "godly woman," I felt I failed to measure up.

A SCRIPTURAL PRECEDENT FOR WORKING WOMEN

Miriam speaks:

Debra is not alone, nor is she unusual. For better or worse, work has been a greater part of a man's identity in the past, and in many Christian circles that continues to be true. Christian women have been discouraged from marketplace work, discouraged from getting a positive sense of identity from having a job outside their homes.

But Christian women *are* in the marketplace now in greater numbers than the general public. Not only are we out there in significant numbers, but most of us *want* to be there. We *like* working, financial necessity aside.

A recent Gallup survey made a similar discovery:

> Working mothers in America view their work as an extremely positive part of their lives. . . . In fact, three-quarters say that they like or love the job they have right now; only 4 percent say that they hate their work.[2]

The truth is women are working with a passion beyond survival. Above the hum of the computers and telephones, above the white noise of offices, classrooms, and hospital hallways, women press on because we believe we are fulfilling God's calling for us—to be women of God in the marketplace, to rub shoulders with co-workers who need the Savior, to be His witnesses wherever He places us.

But privately we are still not completely at peace. We continue to feel inner conflict between the 1950s retro role model of the June Cleaver, totally-devoted, priorities-perfectly-balanced, stay-at-home mom, versus the reality of our lives today. No doubt much of this inner conflict is because we hunger for approval. What Christian does not WISH for the approval of her peers?

Unfortunately, when it comes to who we are at work and at church, the two arenas are frequently at odds. Those surveyed indicated that they did not feel supported by their church and pastor. Less than four in ten full-time working women with children feel affirmed by their pastor or church members for their decision to work.[3]

As Debra interviewed women, she asked, "Do you feel supported by your church?" One mother of three who is back in school pursuing a nursing degree simply sighed and said, "That's a hard one [question] right now. I do [feel supported] in some ways. The deacons responded to my request to visit my parents. The adult education and teaching opportunities are excellent. The church provides great experiences for my kids. But, no, I don't personally feel connected with my church right now."

In other words, the church was there for her when it came to helping aging parents and nurturing children, but for her personally, as she pursued a "calling" to go back to school while raising three kids, the church was not a place she found significant encouragement or support. She had served on numerous boards and committees, volunteered on church task forces, and taught Sunday school. During those times, when she was a full-time mother and active church volunteer, she felt "connected."

When she made the decision to go back to school, when her circumstances changed and she no longer fit the traditional profile, she became a disaffected member—yet even *she* couldn't put a name to why or what caused the shift. She was not a "peripheral" member; she was an active, committed member of a large suburban church. Yet when she broke out of the prescribed mold for Christian women, her sense of connectedness with her church was broken.

On the other hand, a woman with four children, active in her church for more than twelve years and a full-time mom and volunteer, replied to the same question, "Do I feel supported? Oh yes! Very much so. Every time I hear [our minister] preach, he has taught God's Word. I walk out with my bucket feeling full."

Obviously, there are many factors in both of these women's lives that affect their response to an interview question, but their responses are quoted here because they so clearly delineate the continuing dichotomy between working Christian moms and stay-at-home Christian moms. Despite the numbers of Christian women in the workplace, the chasm between women's experience and our theological influences continues to widen, not narrow.

This is both unscriptural and tragic. When we search the Scriptures, rather than finding admonitions to stay home, we find quite the contrary. We find a biblical imperative to do the task(s) God sets before us.

> I know that there is nothing better for [God's people] than to be happy and do good while they live. That [all God's people] may eat and drink, and find satisfaction in all [their] toil—this is the gift of God.
>
> Ecclesiastes 3:12–14

> She considers a field and buys it;
>   out of her earnings she plants a vineyard.
> She sets about her work vigorously;
>   her arms are strong for her tasks.
> She sees that her trading is profitable,
>   and her lamp does not go out at night.
>
> Proverbs 31:16–18

Scripture tells us of women who were tentmakers (Priscilla, Acts 18:2–3), sellers of purple cloth (Lydia, Acts 16:14), realtors (Proverbs 31:16), entrepreneurs of all kinds (Proverbs 31:14). Twenty-one of the thirty-one verses in the last chapter of Proverbs are devoted to a description of a working wife, while applauding the working wife's efforts. "Give her the reward she has earned, and let her works bring her praise at the city gate" (31:31).

We could probably find general consensus in our Christian community that both men and women are to work. Unity ends there. We have found that rational Christian men and women

seem to lose critical thinking skills (in addition to their ability
to listen) when the topic of women's work is raised.

At least two walls of division continue to wreak havoc with
our understanding of women's roles, both in the marketplace
and at home:

- Gender tasks: we disagree on what tasks bring satisfaction to
  men and what tasks bring satisfaction to women.
- Gender priorities: we disagree on what should be male priorities and what should be female priorities when it comes
  to roles at work, church, and home.

After God created male and female, He made a precious pronouncement. He affirmed that His work was good. Diverse and
good, intended for teamwork not competition, intended to enhance not destroy. No matter what the arena, the idea of different sexes was a good one. Unfortunately this difference is too
often the source of tension in the marketplace, at home, and in
our churches. Male/female "stuff" can open the door to bitter-
ness, injustice, and a host of hurts.

Every Christian woman who works out of her home or in
the marketplace is impacted by the powerful gender issues and
religious stereotypes affecting our roles as women. When un-
resolved, gender issues and tensions can shake our faith. In our
dissatisfaction, some messages from radical feminists can start
sounding appealing.

In contrast to the radical feminists, some Christian leaders
advocate that women should be primarily homemakers, a view-
point at the other extreme. Although we see those claims as hu-
manly imposed, religious counterreactions to women entering
the marketplace, the prevalence of that perspective continues to
fuel the "us against them" tensions between stay-at-home moms
and working moms. The continual naysaying of those Christian
leaders critical of Christian women and moms in the market-

place keeps us in the firing line of criticism rather than the community of support.

Whether struggling with religiously sanctioned prejudice or radical feminism, this topic is incredibly important for those of us in the workplace who want God to be God in our lives. Based on research and interviews, we see distortions in theological interpretations sending Christian women to non-Christian sources for support, encouragement, spiritual growth, and affirmation. This "spiritual exodus" is unfortunate and unnecessary when we "correctly handle the word of truth" (2 Timothy 2:15), exposing distortions that keep us from seeing our work from God's point of view. The theological and spiritual implications of these gender issues for women will be addressed again in Chapter 8. For our purposes here, however, let's get back to the workplace. Let's get back to the issue of gender biases and tasks.

WHOSE JOB IS IT?

The following list of jobs and tasks was written in shaky longhand on paper with no wasted margins by a ninety-seven-year-old in 1974.

Some things I have done and helped to do:
All kinds of farm work, including plowing, hoeing, ditching, grubbing, mowing, binding, and cutting grain by hand; stacking wheat, oats, and hay; threshing by hand with a flail made from hickory bushes; breaking and training young horses and mules; feeding and caring for farm animals; blacksmithing and shoeing horses and mules; clearing new ground and burning off same; sawing down trees and helping split them into rails, posts, boards, and shingles; making spokes and ax handles; hauling rails and building miles of rail and stone fences; digging post holes, making gates, bars, doors; sawing, splitting, and hauling wood; making barrels, wagons, and wagon beds; building dry-

kilns of stone and drying pears, apples, and peaches on same; laying foundations, erecting and moving buildings, painting, digging cellars, and carpentering; making maple sugar syrup and sorghum; stripping, cutting, and hauling the cane to the mill.

Doing all kinds of sewing including millinery; mending shoes; taking wool to the carder and spinning the rolls into yarn; weaving, filling quills and shuttles, winding and reeling the yarn into hanks and skeins; cutting carpet rags and helping to warp and put the carpet chain through the sleys; braiding and knitting rugs, stockings, socks, and mittens; crocheting, embroidering, tailoring, and knitting lace.

Taking wheat and corn to mill on horseback; making soap and lye hominy; butchering, rendering lard, curing and canning meat and making sausage; smoking the meat after curing with hickory chips and corn cobs.

Grafting and setting out trees; general orchard work; making cider and vinegar; making apple and peach butter, jellies, jams, preserves; canning all kinds of pickles, relishes, sauces; gathering wild fruits, berries, ginseng, wintergreen, yellow root, and herbs. Raising poultry; bee keeping; assistant P.M. clerk in a department store.

Housework; nursing the sick; washing and dressing the dead.

Hunted and trapped wild animals and game birds. Gathered nuts, gardened, and took many ribbons and prizes at fairs for fresh and canned fruits and vegetables; made comforters, pieced and quilted quilts; picked ducks and geese and made a featherbed and eight pillows.[4]

This list was written by my grandmother, Hatie (Harriet McCoy). As you read through her list, did you think the author was male or female? We often assume that until the women's movement of the 1970s, roles and tasks were clearly defined: men were the breadwinners, women tended the home front. In Christian circles we easily idealized the simplicity and tradi-

tional roles of our grandmother's generation. But Grandma Hatie's list clearly demonstrates that such delineation of roles was
not always the case in years past.

But what about the present? What assumptions do we make
about gender roles?

Conduct your own dinner party survey.

Invite a group of people together for a "work survey." Include an equal number of men and women, some married couples, never married, divorced, and widowed folks. Ask your
guests about tasks of work and employment, the tasks of survival, such as who cleans the house, who puts food on the table,
and maintenance tasks, such as who gets the oil changed or
mows the lawn. Who should do what? Why are more men doing
task X than women and vice versa?

Usually some astute person says that tasks should be done
by whoever is capable of doing them—and everyone agrees, at
least in theory. Somehow it feels unjust to admit otherwise.

So your group decides that either men or women can do any
task. But where does the buck stop if it's not being done right?
Who has ultimate responsibility? In other words, who should
make sure certain tasks get done, regardless of who is *supposed*
to do it?

Who should see that the dams are built so rivers don't drown
people? Who should see that the children are cared for? In our
local paper, any news item about unsupervised children always
comments on the whereabouts of the negligent *mom*. I have
never heard newscasters or writers refer to where the *dad* was.

When I examine Scripture, I discover that tasks are not gender specific; gender biases are not substantiated by our Creator.
I see in Scripture women doing every task known to humankind.
When we are tempted to assume that some tasks are not appropriate for women, remember Paul's words, "Whatever your task,
put yourselves into it, as done for the Lord" (Colossians 3:23,
NRSV).

What can women do? ANYTHING!

What tasks, jobs, or roles are appropriate for women? ANY-THING TO WHICH WE'VE BEEN CALLED.

No task belongs exclusively to females or males.

When I think of the hours spent in debate on what *women* should do and what *men* should do, I wonder if God chuckles and sighs. Or does God perhaps feel angry that His precious humans are debating an insignificant issue in a world with such great needs?

WHAT'S REALLY IMPORTANT?

I think Grandma Hatie's list holds an important truth about gender roles for women today. The true abundant life of a Christian—woman or man—is *not* about who's in charge, where the buck stops, or who is responsible. God's truth is simply that He has a task for each one of us. We are called to obey His call rather than question, *Who? Why?* or *Is it my job?*

We are further entangling the gender jungle when we endorse or advocate female should's that so easily contribute to false guilt. For example, if we find ourselves thinking, *I'd be a better mom if I stayed at home,* unwittingly we're participating in the very gender bias with which we struggle.

While browsing in a Christian bookstore, Debra ran into a woman from her church. Having both recently completed writing projects, their conversation quickly turned to what they anticipated doing next. After listening to the woman for several minutes, Debra bluntly said, "You know, if you were a man and said what you've just said, I'd ask you, 'Why aren't you going to seminary?' Everything you've just described sounds like you're called to the ministry, but you're not letting yourself think of that as a possibility."

When we fail to recognize the truth that God will use whomever He has available, given the ability He has created within each person, we are shortchanging God and ourselves. Those decisions are His alone, not ours.

As sisters in the body of Christ, when we see women with abundant lives like Hatie, what message do we send them? Ask yourself:

- Do I encourage them to thank God that they are able to toil, that they have health and strength?
- Do I acknowledge and affirm any part they have in subduing the earth (as God commands in Genesis 1:26), whether that part seems big or small?
- Am I suffocating their abundant life with people-designed false guilt?
- Am I encouraging and supporting the "Haties" among us?

Recognizing our own prejudices is not easy. As we ask ourselves these questions, we may consider ourselves open-minded, progressive, supportive of women pursuing nontraditional roles. But we're not going to let you off the hook so easily. Let's look at a controversial example. What about women in combat?

Some critics of women serving in combat have opposed their participation by drawing a correlation between violence against women and women in combat. I believe it requires mental gymnastics to put the issue of women in combat in the same category as violence against women. A woman as protector is a role filled by Deborah the prophetess and Miriam, Moses' sister.

In the fourth chapter of Judges, we learn that Deborah was "leading Israel at that time" (v. 4). She went to battle with her army and gave the command of when to attack (vv. 4–14).

The woman, Jael, killed General Sisera, a mission Jabin's army had not been able to accomplish (vv. 1–27). Her victory is an example of God using His people with the skills they have developed in ordinary circumstances. Women were in charge of pitching the tents in that day. Jael, being handy with tent pegs, drove one through Sisera's head. The honor of conquest went to a woman that day as Deborah had predicted.

Scripture is clear that God has called women to many tasks that Christians today often consider "nontraditional." Such stories challenge our thinking about whose "traditions" we are supposed to follow in order to be godly women. Not only was Deborah leading Israel (a challenge to traditional beliefs in the church that women are not called to leadership), but this story also teaches us that some women are (1) gifted by God with the skills and abilities for combat, (2) called by God to function in combat. To exclude women from combat denies the facts of Scripture and adds to the Word of God.

Certainly, moving into combat positions raises women's earning potential and opens new avenues for advancement in the armed forces. I would wish that any woman could apply and compete for any military assignment, even if that assignment requires combat, if her motivation and skills are equal to the task.

Just as I sense the call of God to work in the public schools and be "salt and light" there, many women may sense the call of God to assume combat positions in our armed forces, representing God wherever they are. The church should not deny them their calling.

WHAT DIFFERENCE DOES IT MAKE?

Allowing God to direct and enable any woman to do any job speaks to many issues in the Christian community. We are continually surprised at how readily many Christians, both men and women, wish to dismiss gender inequities, biases, and undercurrents. We either fall into the ever-present temptation to put God on trial for fairness when we face challenges of gender injustice, or we simply throw up our hands, sigh, and tell ourselves, "That's just the way it is." Or worse, we deny any problem exists.

Debra interviewed an accomplished woman in her fifties who has served in countless leadership positions, managed multimillion-dollar budgets, and acted as a change agent both in her church and community. She still describes her primary role as a caregiver for her husband and family. During her interview regarding women's roles, Adrian minimized any gender-based difficulties or challenges she has confronted when serving on predominately male boards.

"Very few times have I ever felt condescended to," Adrian said thoughtfully. "I go in assuming the men I'll be working with are broad thinkers. Healthy men have no problem dealing with women who are decision makers; they have more problems dealing with women who are fluff!"

However, she went on to describe "the most extreme example of men 'persecuting' women" in her experience, a situation involving several male colleagues who opposed her efforts to change the manner in which an organization complied with tax laws. She detailed an almost unbelievable tale of institutional blackballing, harassing phone calls in the middle of the night, and an attempt to involve her husband in a compromising situation—all because they opposed her efforts to change the status quo. The fact is, little opposition would have surfaced had a man been championing the change. If this was the most extreme example, what was the norm that she simply tolerated or overlooked?

Dismissal. Denial. Fatalistic despair. Defeatist acquiescence. None of these is an effective response. As Christians, as women, we can do better than that. We can be change agents. We can be workplace missionaries.

Dr. Laura Schlessinger, Ph.D. and host of a nationally syndicated radio program, says unabashedly, "Contrary to much of the feminist cant, there are many things we can learn from men's perspective about life and personal identity . . . there is no realization of dreams and purpose for either women or men without difficulty, opposition, disappointment, and failure. . . . In order to grow, you've got to face the fact that painless change happens only in fairy tales."[5]

Painless change happens only in fairy tales. How true. We need not be told our work world has changed. We work in new spaces doing tasks our mothers and grandmothers never dreamed of, solving problems for issues that did not exist twenty years ago, using technology only on drawing boards ten years ago. We know our world has changed. We're also aware that attitudes, role expectations, and gender undercurrents are slow to change—even within ourselves. The tension between the opposing forces is where the tug-of-war of the heart begins. "There is a tendency in us to want to live tension free. But . . . I believe that this tension is God's gift to us. . . . I believe that our creative energies are activated by just that kind of upsetting tension. It is in responding to this gnawing discomfort that we have the possibility of giving shape to dreams that are at once faithful to who we are and who we can become."[6]

How do we live in delicate balance with the inner tension? How do we effect change? How do we make a difference? Read on. That's what *Shattering Our Assumptions* is all about.

NOTES

1. Out of respect for the author, his name has been changed.
2. Carin Rubenstein, "The Confident Generation," *Working Mother* (May 1994), p. 38.
3. "Today's Christian Woman and Work," in-magazine survey, p. 2.
4. Miriam Neff, *Sisters of the Heart* (Nashville: Thomas Nelson, 1995), pp. 14–17. (Partial list appears here; entire list appears in *Sisters of the Heart*.)
5. Laura Schlessinger, Ph.D., *Ten Stupid Things Women Do to Mess Up Their Lives* (New York: HarperPerennial, 1995), pp. 6–7.

6. Paula Ripple, *Growing Strong at Broken Places* (Notre Dame, Ind.: Ave Maria Press, 1986), quoted from *A Guide to Prayer for All God's People* (Nashville: Upper Room Books, 1990), p. 256.

Three

The Juggling Game

Miriam speaks:

Friday night, 7:30 P.M. Oakbrook, Illinois, 1984. I sat at my computer oblivious to the minutes passing. How could these two appraisals be so far apart? Do I order a third? There goes some of the profit margin. Will the client company cover the difference between what the transferring employee wants for his house and these appraised values?

I lean back and straighten the skirt of my Brooks Brothers suit (my wardrobe "I'm professional" statement that year.)

In a suburb thirty-five minutes away three young boys ages six, eight, and ten gather with their thirteen-year-old sister and Dad around a cardboard-boxed dinner—pizza again.

Something's wrong with this picture, I thought. And it's not the discrepancy between the appraisals. How deep and how wide can the wedge of work divide my family? I typed an e-mail message about the appraisals to the account manager, turned off my terminal, and headed for home.

I had not intended to work so late, but it was happening with frequent regularity. Work had become an all-consuming presence crowding out relationships, relaxation, and things I never intended to give up.

As I turned onto the tollway toward home that night, I determined I would not work on Friday nights again, even if it meant changing jobs.

PUTTING WORK IN ITS PLACE

Can women become addicted to their jobs? Slim chance, we might have guessed a decade ago. Workaholics are men, not women. Men are the competitors, obsessively climbing the career ladders, scrapping for promotions. Women are too relationship oriented to worry about work. Women have obsessions. Women have addictions. But not in the marketplace.

Times have changed.

If workaholism was a male malady in the postwar era while our nation was becoming industrialized, an era when many women worked at home while men worked in the marketplace, it is not true today. While women may have been less likely than men to idolize their work in the past, the winds are changing, and the temptation is already upon us. As women enter the marketplace in increasing numbers, we face the eternal struggle of choosing not just between good and evil, but between good and better, better and best.

"Many of us would not initially define ourselves as workaholics," says author Anne Wilson Schaef. "However, there are many of us who do too much, keep too busy, spend all our time taking care of others and, in general, do not take care of ourselves."[1]

Work can sit on the throne of our life. Our job can be our master, our career the commander of our hours, thoughts, and dreams. We never intend it so. Distortions creep in while we are busy, distracted, and energized by good intentions. Priorities are easily confused.

The god of work promises women four excellent rewards. Each reward is good, and there's nothing wrong with wanting all four:

- The satisfaction of success.
- The security of a paycheck.
- The affirmation of accomplishment.
- The status of having nice things.

What woman does not want satisfaction, security, affirmation, and status? Success on a job brings satisfaction. A paycheck brings security. Being recognized for our accomplishments brings affirmation of our abilities and an enhanced sense of self-esteem. And the status of owning nice things: oh, those exquisitely tailored clothes, heady perfumes, luscious fabrics, beautifully decorated surroundings, smooth-purring automobiles—undoubtedly those make us feel good. . . . Yes, work will deliver it all, or so the myth would have us believe. The problem is not in wanting the rewards of a successful career; the problem comes in losing perspective.

It has been said that we worship our work, work at our play, and play at our worship. Is work an idol in our life? We must work to live, but do we, without recognition, slip over the line and live to work?

"No, not me. I'm a Christian," we may say to ourselves.

But deep within us in moments of blunt honesty, we know that we are wooed. We know we are vulnerable. The seduction of work is subtle. Many of us are tempted. Misplaced priorities begin with common, believable distortions of truth, distortions that even Christian women can believe.

If I don't do this, it won't get done.

I know I'm overcommitted right now, but this project is important.

I know I haven't spent much time with my kids this week, but we'll do something special this weekend.

I'll have more time after I get this job done.

Sound familiar? These are the mythical distortions of women who do too much; women who think no one else can do something as well as they can.

How do we know when we are falling prey to worshiping our work? How do we recognize when work is taking over, confusing our priorities and turning us into candidates for Workaholics Anonymous? If not workaholics, are we "busyaholics," "rushaholics," "churchaholics"? How do we know when projects, commitments, and responsibilities should be honored and completed, or questioned and re-evaluated? When do we say no, even though the request for our time and effort is worthwhile and valuable?

THE TYRANNY OF THE CLOCK
Debra speaks:

"Katy, get your coat on NOW! Kari, shoes. Shoes are the priority, not picking out what toy you want to take to church. We have to be out the door in three minutes. Come on, let's get into high gear!"

I was literally barking orders.

"Katy, brush your teeth. Kari, your dirty clothes don't belong on my bed. Katy, I'm sorry, but orange headband, purple socks, and red sweater are not acceptable for church. Try again."

A typical Sunday morning in the Klingsporn household. Frenzied. Three females tripping over each other in the bathroom. "Monster Mom's" admonitions, followed by tears and frustration.

"But Mom, this is all I can find. Nothing else is clean!" comes Katy's predictable response.

You know you've made an impression (and perhaps used a certain tone of voice too often) when you overhear your daughters telling their dolls, "Do it NOW!"

I'm the wife of a minister. We belong to a great church. And I hated Sunday mornings.

Because of my husband's responsibilities, he always went early. I became parent-on-duty when it came to getting the girls out the door to church on time. I could picture my girls' mental image of their Sunday morning mom: fangs, snarling, hair on end, a witchy-woman voice. Sunday mornings were not fun in our house.

As we drove the two miles to church one Sunday morning in complete silence, I found myself wondering, *What's more important? Getting to church on time—no matter how grumpy the morning becomes to make that happen? Or making happy memories? Making Sunday mornings something we all look forward to?*

Then I remembered Jesus' words to the Pharisees, "The Sabbath was made for man, not man for the Sabbath" (Mark 2:27).

Hmmm. Perhaps I was valuing the wrong thing. Why was it so important to get to church on time? My kids are growing up as preacher's kids; they are now and probably always will be PK's. They spend more time in church in one year than most kids do in ten.

I broke the silence as we drove the remaining few blocks.

"Katy, Kari. I've made a decision. Are you listening?" I asked softly. "We won't do this again. We won't turn our Sunday mornings into yucky, grumpy, short-tempered snarlies just to get out the door. You two are more important to me than getting to church on time. From now on, if we're late, we're late. No big deal. We're going to make our Sunday mornings fun for all of us. I'm sorry I was such a monster mom this morning."

That grumpy Sunday morning was more than two years ago. We've held to our resolve. Now on Sunday mornings we take extra time for snuggles. We don't get bent out of shape over what's clean and what's not; whatever is in closets and drawers, that's what gets worn. And most of all, we don't have last-minute scrambles to get out the door. We don't drive to church angry, frustrated, and upset. And, amazingly, more often than not we actually make it on time. The problem wasn't in trying to get out the door on time. The problem was what took priority.

Whether we consider ourselves workaholics or not, few women are immune to the everyday stresses of juggling priorities. When the clock in the room assumes the importance of dictator rather than a simple record-keeping device for the time of day, the disease may have struck.

Literally every woman we interviewed feels the press for time, the rigors of demanding schedules, the lack of time for self, and the need or desire for more time with her spouse.

Biblically we are commanded to have no idols, no other gods before God. "You shall have no other gods before me" (Exodus 20:3). In today's world most of us don't get into a golden calf thing. We're not much for graven images. What does that commandment mean to us as working women, Christian moms, committed churchgoers? Is there something in the first commandment that applies to juggling demands and priorities, something to help us wrestle with the tensions between priorities and inner tugs-of-war?

FIRST THINGS FIRST
Miriam speaks:

Always an appropriate place to begin, Debra and I start with opening our Bibles to examine our own hearts and lives. We look for answers to the questions of priorities. We ask what our work means to God, what we are instructed to do with our 100+ pound bodies of muscle and mind.

> Then I realized that it is good and proper for a woman to eat and drink, and to find satisfaction in her toilsome labor under the sun during the few days of life God has given her—for this is her lot. Moreover, when God gives any woman wealth and possessions, and enables her to enjoy them, to accept her lot and be happy in her work—this

is a gift of God. She seldom reflects on the days of her life, because God keeps her occupied with gladness of heart.

Ecclesiastes 5:18–20,
with female nouns/pronouns

Are we occupied with "gladness of heart"? Or does juggling our multiple roles at work, home, and church give us reason to reach for the Extra-Strength Tylenol?

Author Keith Miller suggests a simple exercise to evaluate what we idolize, or in other words, what we are putting at the center of our lives.[2]

"What is the first thing you think of when you awake, the last thing you find yourself thinking of as you go to sleep?" Keith asks. "What comes to mind in idle moments, when you're running errands, stuck in traffic, or sitting quietly?"

Whatever involuntarily occupies our thoughts is a good clue as to what we idolize, what we allow to occupy the throne of our life. Granted, everyone goes through unusually busy times, times when we let the laundry slide, forget to pay a bill, or overlook an appointment. These are not the indicators to which Keith is referring. His question challenges us to look at consistent patterns. Ask yourself these questions:

- Am I too busy to pray?
- Am I frequently too busy to exercise or take time for myself?
- Am I often short-tempered with my close friends, spouse, and/or children?
- Am I frequently tired and resentful?
- Am I able to enjoy recreational activities, or do I worry about projects, deadlines, and commitments?

If you answered yes to more than one of these questions, chances are priorities are squeezed. What you value is at odds with where your time is committed. Perhaps it's time to look at whether or not how we use our time is in alignment with what we truly value. If the two aren't in sync, the inner tugs-of-war intensify and we may be ready for a commitment overhaul.

Do the Next Thing

Debra speaks:

When my days seem overwhelming, burdensome, or downright toilsome, I remember Jesus' words, "Come to me, all you who are weary and burdened, and I will give you rest. Take my yoke upon you, and learn from me, for I am gentle . . . and you will find rest for your souls" (Matthew 11:28–29).

What does Jesus mean when He tells us to "come to me"? First, Christ is telling us that we can't do it alone. If we want God to be God in our lives, priorities included, we need to come to Him.

As I read of woman after woman in the Bible, God was never uncaring of their work, their labors, their toil. Often a woman's work is included in her description: Priscilla, Miriam, Deborah, Esther, Ruth, all were described in their real-life struggles. When women in the Bible were up against a wall, the solutions to their distress were found in following God's direction. Ruth was desperate. No husband. No food. An aging mother-in-law to feed and care for. Ruth lived in the days before women wore pantyhose and tailored suits or earned college degrees. She couldn't exactly apply at the local temp service. She trusted God and God provided, but only as she did the next thing. She wasn't given a complete set of directions in a divine handbook. She was told simply to do the next thing.

How many times have I looked at the commitments before me, feeling completely stressed-out, afraid I'll never get it all done, questioning how I let myself get into "circuit overload" *again,* and over a cup of coffee in the quiet darkness of an early morning, I've prayed:

Lord, what do I do? How am I going to get it all done? I'm overwhelmed, tired, and I don't even know where to start.

As I sit in the darkness, taking comfort from the black richness of strong coffee, I get an idea, or I realize I have to get my kids off to school before I can do anything else, or words that I couldn't come up with the day before begin bubbling in my mind and I know the writing will progress. In other words, in prayer we're often given direction through a still, quiet voice within, a voice we often can't hear over the clamor of mental "to-do" lists, phone calls, car radios, and workday realities.

Some of the most comforting, helpful words I've heard were spoken by a friend who simply said, "Deb, you just have to do the next thing. I know you. I know you'll get it all done. But for now, just do the next thing."

Do the next thing.

Sometimes the best way to reduce the stress we feel is as simple as these three things:

- Evaluate priorities.
- Pray.
- Do the next thing.

No Room for Idols

Miriam speaks:

Let's go back for a few moments to the four rewards we gain from working and ask ourselves if perhaps we need an attitude adjustment in one of those four arenas.

1. The Satisfaction of Success

Debra and I have both been tempted to believe that success in our jobs will bring us ultimate satisfaction. We have been guilty of letting work become too important, letting work-related goals and aspirations dominate our time, energy, and efforts. We have felt at times that God is unaware or uncaring of our workplace conflicts or our struggles to keep our priorities in the right place. We've wrestled with questioning how relevant our faith is to our work.

"No temptation has seized you except what is common to man [and woman]" (1 Corinthians 10:13).

These temptations are not unique to us, nor are they new. The age-old success seduction began in the Garden of Eden. That beautiful piece of fruit was appealing, useful, and would serve a valuable end—or so it seemed to Eve. To eat the fruit would increase her knowledge, enhance her personal power, and raise her level of achievement. How easily we justify our efforts to succeed.

Yet as Christian women, we have different criteria for success. We are called to be faithful. How simple. All we need to be is authentic followers. We are not called to achieve a certain level of affluence. We are not called to any particular level of accomplishment or recognition. We are called to be faithful. When we are obedient to our Creator, success by work or career standards may or may not come. But that, dear sisters, is unimportant. What *God* thinks counts.

2. The Source of Our Security

Do you feel stressed out by a slim bank account? Do you eagerly anticipate the next payday more than any other day? Consider the following:

> I am not saying this because I am in need, for I have learned to be content whatever the circumstances. I know what it is to be in need, and I know what it is to have plenty. I have learned the secret of being content in any and every situation, whether well fed or hungry, whether living in plenty or in want. I can do everything through him who gives me strength.
>
> Philippians 4:11–13

When I am tempted to doubt God's goodness because I see financial discrepancies and injustice in my workplace, I remember the parable Jesus told about work. He told of people who worked different amounts of time, and yet, at the end of the day they all received the same paycheck. The employer in the parable gave a perspective that sounds politically incorrect today: "Don't I have the right to do what I want with my own money? Or are you envious because I am generous? So the last will be first, and the first will be last" (Matthew 20:15–16).

We take our need to God. It is unnecessary and inappropriate to tell Him how to meet our need. He is, after all, God.

3. The Affirmation of Accomplishment

When the stuff of life feels important to our happiness, we are vulnerable to idolizing work. Won't we be promoted if we work harder? Won't we earn better perks? Our paychecks will be bigger; our purchases will have "real class." And we will feel affirmed.

Does this sound familiar?

Christian women have a guaranteed source of affirmation. Consider the following:

> Whom have I in heaven but you? And being with you,
> I desire nothing on earth.
>
> Psalm 73:25

> You are my portion, O Lord; I have promised to obey
> your words.
>
> Psalm 119:57

Affirmation from people—co-workers, employers, friends, family—is great. But ultimately, only God's affirmation is guaranteed. And that's enough.

4. The Status of Having Nice Things

Consider for a moment the people in your life who are your most comfortable companions. Why are you comfortable around them? Is it because of what they are wearing? Or the value of their surroundings, whether home, apartment, or condominium? Chances are your comfort level with your companions is related to who they are and your relationship to them, not their stuff.

How long do you feel wonderful in something new? How long does the thrill of a new vehicle last? How easily we conform to the commercials! When we buy into "stuff status," I think we insult our Creator. He is Creator, Distributor, and Redistributor—all with His own unique purposes and goals. To believe any less is to call Him god, not God. For God to be our God is status enough.

CAUGHT IN THE CURRENT OF CHANGE

We've looked at several factors that contribute to workplace stress: gender issues, when work becomes too important, conflicts in priorities, and the universal time squeeze with which women contend. There is another factor that is a big player contributing to workplace stress. The 38 percent of the women surveyed identifying workplace stress as a significant dimension of their lives are caught in the swift current of social change.

Consider the implications for employment. Door-to-door salespeople are replaced by telemarketers. Mall shopping can be replaced by internet shopping, replacing cashiers with microchips. Health care by professional diagnosis is being replaced by health care as per what the HMO manual dictates will be paid for. As rapidly as jobs are changing, families are changing too. Women are caught in the current.

As a counselor in a public high school, I interact with hundreds of teens and frequently meet with parents. This week I had a parent conference I wish wouldn't have been necessary.

A Christian mom and fourteen-year-old student sat in my office, the mom never anticipating what I was going to say to her when I asked her to come to school on her lunch break from work.

"Your daughter has asked me to tell you she is pregnant."

As the three of us sat together in my office, my heart agonized equally for this mother and daughter. A fourteen-year-old child who would soon parent a child, a mom who had been handed a life-changing, never-forever-the-same crisis.

Imagine the family discussion between Mom, daughter, and Dad that night after our mother/daughter meeting in my office. Imagine the dark quiet after Amy left with her boyfriend. Imagine the anger and blaming between parents, the hurt, and eventual silence as they struggled to make sense of this situation. Imagine Amy's mom at work the next day trying to "just work."

I sometimes lean against a counter in the student cafeteria in those noisy minutes before the bell, watching hundreds of teens milling around, pushing, grabbing book bags, some asking for attention, others hiding in the crowd. I look at the almost women and wonder what surprises life will spring on them.

Change is inevitable. Change is unavoidable. Change is stressful. And times are definitely changing. But for young women, the changes are even more profound. The high school scene for our daughters is drastically different from the experience of our sons.

Statistics are the same, whether looking at professing Christians or the general public: 40 percent of our teenage girls now experience pregnancy. Four out of every ten girls will face the same dilemma Amy faced. The meeting I had with Amy's mother dealt with a situation I see all too frequently.

Consider other changes women face:

- Each young woman who chooses to marry faces a 50-percent chance that the marriage will be dissolved.
- Divorce brings a 73-percent reduction in a woman's disposable income, compared to a 46-percent increase for the man involved.

Whether through divorce, job loss, family crises, or any number of other radical changes that turn our world upside down, change is one of the biggest sources of stress for working women. Change is a fact of life and can be either positive or negative.

Christian women today change careers, change jobs, change marital status, and a host of other roles. Some we control (at least from our human perspective); some are beyond our control, our dreams, our wishes, or even what we believe we can survive!

Facing change and living through and beyond it is like closing a messy, disorganized file drawer. First you have to sort categories and straighten "stuff" before you can slide it shut.

When facing change we have to sort through our attitudes and understand our past in a new way. We need to reflect on the influences that have shaped our lives. In trying to redefine our roles to accommodate new challenges, we remember what we've learned from those closest to us—parents, siblings, aunts, uncles, grandparents, close friends. We think about what our spiritual beliefs and experiences have been. We consider important institutions in our past and the messages they sent us. With all this "stuff" and with a great deal of emotional, spiritual, and relational "sorting," we face change.

When I knew I needed to change jobs, I was unsuccessful at even getting interviews where I wanted to work. I could see positives in the kind of work (educator/counselor) I wanted, but doors seemed closed in the schools where I wanted to work. I did not see God's *timing* and *process*, two significant blind spots for me during that time. Even though I couldn't see God at work, I clung tenaciously to scriptural truth, trusting that God was at work in my life, doing a new thing (Isaiah 43:19), something I did not expect. I saw the positive match between the job requirements and my abilities; I saw the negative closed doors;

and I couldn't understand why I was not getting the job I wanted.

In hindsight (and mine is better than average!), I see that God honed me by placing me in two schools that were not of my choosing. Although the experiences were challenging and at times difficult, I sure learned a lot and gained invaluable experience. (My office in one school had a bullet hole in the window—comforting reminder.).

Change is a reality for every one of us. Although it is beyond the scope of this book to address the specifics of coping with change, we do want to offer a tool we use to regain our perspective when too many changes seem to be coming our way too quickly.

Take a few minutes and imagine you have the opportunity to sit face-to-face with Jesus for an hour. He asks you how things are going, and you tell Him about the changes in your life, where you feel the greatest tension, and what causes you the greatest stress. After that conversation, how would you complete the following sentences?

Jesus would look at my situation and see the following positives:

_____

_____

_____

_____

Jesus would look at my situation and see the following negatives:

_____

_____

_____

A possible blind spot I face as I deal with these changes is

_____

_____

_____

("Blind spot" means an unknown, something we can't see or understand entirely, a situation in which we know some of the before and after, but the middle is a surprise. Our blind spots are those factors that limit our perspective or understanding.)

Next, with Bible in hand, think of verses that are meaningful to you. Ask friends or your pastor for verses that are particularly relevant to your situation. We have copied verses onto 3×5 cards and into our journals and carried them with us during stressful times. Are there any verses that relate to your situation? Then complete the following statement:

I believe, based on the following verse(s),

_____

_____

_____

that God's perspective on the unknown is

_____

You may find several verses related to the unknown you face. As you write what Scripture says about these blind spots, you will find your Creator mentoring you. As Laura Schlessinger says, "Painless change happens only in fairy tales." But change is the avenue to growth, wisdom, and spiritual depth. We discover new truths about our Creator and come to know ourselves better through change.

Paul told Christians almost two thousand years ago that difficulty, pain, and tests of our faith were to be expected. When our tests are neither what we expected nor what we feel strong enough to face, our Creator assures us that He is faithful and will not let us be tested beyond what we can bear (1 Corinthians 10:13). His promise to women in changing times and crisis times is the same: He will provide a way for us to withstand whatever we are called to face.

OFFERING OUR WORK, NOT IDOLIZING OUR WORK

I was encouraged to see in the results of my research that Christian women working in the marketplace KNOW they are fulfilling God's calling for them. Our reality matches Frederick Buechner's theological definition of the word "vocation":

> Vocation. It comes from the Latin *vocare*, to call, and means the work a [woman] is called to by God. . . . The place God calls you to is the place where your deep gladness and the world's deep hunger meet.[3]

Our deep gladness and the world's deep hunger. Our work is the arena in which we live King Solomon's inspired words that

God gives us work and wishes us satisfaction in our labor (Ecclesiastes 5:18–20).

A large percentage of the women in my survey see their workplace as the place to do what God has created them to do. As working Christian women, we are living the Scripture that tells us, "Whatever you do, work at it with all your heart, as working for the Lord, not for [people]" (Colossians 3:23).

We may feel exhausted, our emotions may be stressed, our hours stretched. But above it all, we hear God calling.

Work is called work because it's *work*—not a day in the park, not a Caribbean vacation. Work is toilsome, even in the best of circumstances. But it's also more. Work is where our deep gladness and the world's deep hunger meet.

I am encouraged by the mission potential of increasing numbers of women in the marketplace. The workplace will be the most important place in the days ahead for people to hear who God is. The worker by our side may be the one who needs to hear the Good News of Jesus Christ. We can be God's voice and hands where the rubber meets the road of real-life issues and day-to-day struggles.

My friend Gail introduced a member of her computer software team to Jesus. In the pain of his divorce, he trusted Gail and knew she cared. When she spoke of her source of comfort, he listened.

I talked to one of my students this week about God's desire to comfort her after three of her relatives had died in an automobile accident. She questioned why such a thing could happen and where God was in the midst of her sorrow. She was comfortable with me. She felt safe. She could be open about her feelings. She asked me if I believed God were really good. Where did I have this opportunity to speak about God's unfailing love? On my job.

While my passion has not diminished for the workplace to be more family friendly, gender equal, and just for women—and

I will continue to be an advocate for those issues—I have a far greater workplace passion: to be God's witness. In order to be God's witness on the job, I've got to let God be God in my life—and that means work can't be my idol. When it comes to priorities, stress, perspective, and change, one thing I know without fail: God is in control. I'm here for His purposes.

NOTES

1. Anne Wilson Schaef, *Meditations for Women Who Do Too Much* (San Francisco: Harper & Row, 1990), p. 3.
2. Keith Miller suggested the exercise during a lecture at Colonial Church of Edina, Minnesota.
3. Frederick Buechner, *Wishful Thinking: A Theological ABC* (New York: HarperSanFrancisco, 1973), p. 95.

Part Two

Women Away From Work

"My God will meet all your needs according to his glorious riches in Christ Jesus."

Philippians 4:19

"If I find in myself a desire which no experience in this world can satisfy, the most probable explanation is that I was made for another world."

C. S. Lewis

Four

Women and Money:
Statistics, Stress, and Dollars and Cents

ebra speaks:

Dthe knock on the door came at an inconvenient time. I was trying to get dressed and out the door, running characteristically late.

"Do you have a phone?" came the question from a surprisingly young face. Not, "Can I use your phone?" She didn't presume.

"Yeah, sure," I said, surprised that anyone *wouldn't* have a phone.

"Uh, our phone don't work. Can I make a call? My baby's sick and I gotta take her to the clinic. It won't take long. Here, I got a quarter."

I'm an incurable people watcher. Shameless might be a better description. No matter where I am, who I'm with, or what I'm doing, I always watch people and wonder who they are, what their lives are like. I'm always the one who notices when friends and acquaintances get new eyeglasses or a haircut. I observe, I remember, I notice details.

Given my fascination with people watching, I find it rather curious that I had lived across the street from the same family for a year and a half and never really noticed them, never really questioned what their lives were like.

Each day as I left for work wearing the tasteful attire of a young career woman on the rise, I would see her standing at the street corner, juggling bundles, bags, and backpack. I never paid much attention to her. We didn't speak, avoided eye contact, and maintained by mutual consent the invisible barrier separating our worlds. I didn't wonder where she was going, didn't question her age, and didn't imagine what her life was like. She was one of those peripheral people who fill city streets, nameless faces living an invisible desperation.

My husband and I were living in a small one-bedroom rental house in an area of town unsafe in which to walk alone at night. Six blocks away were abandoned buildings, knifings, robberies, and rapes. Our neighborhood was one of deteriorating houses, rusted cars, and long-neglected yards. But rent was cheap and with my husband in graduate school ("in dissertation" as his professors would say), a small house in a run-down neighborhood near the university was all our budget could handle. I was in the "young upstart" stage of a publishing career—long on goals and ambition, short on cash.

I lived across the street from this young woman standing at my door, but our lives were worlds apart. I left a poor neighborhood each day, knowing my stay there was temporary, a means to an end. She was a permanent resident.

Her name was Carol Elkins. Her long, stringy hair needed to be washed. She wore jeans sized for a woman twenty pounds thinner.

"The phone is over there, on the other side of the bed," I said as she timidly followed me into our bedroom.

She quickly made the call, humbly said her thank-you's, and left. Thus began the intersection of our lives. She was no longer anonymous. She was now a neighbor. Carol and her younger sister, Paula, began to come over several times a week to use the phone. In a house as small as ours, privacy wasn't an option. Over a period of time, my husband and I began to piece together bits of information about their lives.

I had assumed Carol and I were about the same age. Not so. She was nearly ten years younger than I, a teenage mother with two children, a high school dropout. The rough-looking man living in their house as her mother's on-again, off-again lover wasn't her father. Our lives were very different.

I had options. She had responsibilities. I had a future filled with promise. Her future looked grim.

"Is your husband a preacher or somethin'?" Carol asked one day as she came in to use the phone.

"Well, kind of," I said, trying to figure out if it was worth explaining that he was in graduate school, not seminary.

"Yeah, I seen y'all leavin' your house on Sunday mornin's, all dressed up and stuff. I figured your husband must be a preacher. Y'all sure do have a lot of Bibles."

She had noticed our desk and bookshelves. Yes, they were lined with Bibles. You couldn't walk through our front door without noticing the bookshelf—it was the largest piece of furniture we owned. We were now typecast. We were now *that preacher and his wife across the street.* Carol and her sister treated us respectfully, deferentially, never calling us by name and only hesitantly making eye contact.

At 8:30 A.M. one Tuesday morning, the doorbell rang. Paula stood outside our door, alone, timid, and anxious. This time Carol wasn't with her sister.

"Could you help us?" Paula asked, her voice fearful. "Carol's in jail. Can you do anything?"

My husband began gently asking questions, calming Paula simply by his kindness. Slowly the details emerged.

About a year before, Carol had been caught trying to shoplift baby clothes from a nearby Kmart. She had been fined, given a suspended sentence, and placed on probation for a year. All she had to do was make restitution payments and report to her probation officer. For six months Carol had followed the terms of her probation faithfully. But in time, she grew to dislike her probation officer, who treated her with contempt and derision. As their relationship became increasingly adversarial, she left the probation meetings feeling humiliated. Carol's solution to the difficulty was simple, but not legal. She stopped going to her probation officer. She simply quit reporting. She violated the terms of her probation, not by committing further crimes, but by failing to report to the probation department. Four months later she sat in jail, homesick, worried about her two infant children, with her sixteen-year-old sister coming to us for help because neither of them knew what else to do.

"Can you do anything?"

They had come to our door time and again to use the phone, look up something in our Yellow Pages, or borrow some sugar. Now a sixteen-year-old girl stood on our front step, frantic that her older sister was in jail, a sister only two years older but who filled a mother's role and watched out for her. Paula and Carol didn't know us well, but we were *that preacher and his wife across the street.*

My husband was a Ph.D. candidate in biblical studies, not social work. *Could we help?* Only if a doctoral thesis were put on hold for a day—I had to go to work. As I walked out the door and my eyes met his, I knew he would help. I knew his day would be spent making phone calls, tracking down information, reassuring two young girls who were enmeshed in a legal system that confused and frightened them. Functionally illiterate, they knew nothing of the legal process, the consequences of failing to report, or the steps to acquiring legal assistance.

The week that followed was an education for my husband and me. His was a week of visits to the legal aid society, probation department, county jail, and bail bondsmen. We learned details about this family across the street that we'd rather have not known. Carol and Paula lived in a two-bedroom house with their mother, their mother's lover, and two younger preteen sisters. Carol's mother had an infant, fathered by the man currently living with them. Carol's younger child had been fathered by her mother's lover—and sixteen-year-old Paula was pregnant by the same man! The winter before Carol's legal difficulties began, when I first noticed her standing on the street corner waiting for the bus, she was making frequent visits to the public health clinic because they had no heat or hot water in their house. Food was scarce, clothes were dirty, and their home was a roach and pest haven. After living across the street from Carol Elkins, statistics have never again been cold, impersonal numbers. For many women, the odds are against them.

THE STAGGERING REALITIES

Miriam speaks:

Carol's story is only one young woman's story behind staggering statistics. When we look at the issues impacting young women and their income-earning potential, the world scene isn't too encouraging:

- By the year 2000 more children will be born in our country to women without husbands than to married women.[1]
- Forty percent of American women believe the world is too bad a place in which to bring babies,[2] but babies are being born to teenage mothers at an alarming rate (28 percent of births in 1990 were to unmarried women, and the rate of increase is accelerating).[3]
- It is all but impossible for a high school dropout who gives birth to her first baby by age nineteen to be anything but poor.
- One in three adolescents confronts alcohol and drug prob-

lems or physical or sexual abuse in the home.
- Seventy percent of teenage mothers were sexually abused before they entered the teen years, abuse which typically occurs
  in their home by a relative or friend of a relative.[4]

Debra's neighborhood experience with Carol Elkins brought
the statistics to her front door. My work with teens in an urban
high school brings the stark reality of these statistics into my
office on a daily basis.

The list of facts that impact the material worth of a woman
is quite long. Statistics tell us that many women do not have the
luxury of daydreaming, goal setting, or career choices. The great
majority of women today are daily fighting a struggle to survive.
I believe that it is important for us to keep this big picture before
us when we talk about women, their families and finances.

Contrary to frequent sermons Christians hear admonishing
us not to lay up our stores on earth, or reminding us of the rich
man who kept acquiring more stuff, for many women the real
scenario is the poor woman whose oil jar was nearly empty and
she began to fear starvation for herself and her son (2 Kings 4:1–
7). Rather than idolizing money and the comforts it affords,
many women are concerned that they may not have enough to
keep a roof overhead and bread on the table.

Women and money. Whether we have a lot, a little, or live
somewhere in between, money has a significant impact on our
lives. Even for women like Debra and me, women who live educated, comfortable, middle-class lives, financial concerns are
an ongoing issue.

A photocopied cartoon hanging in an office seemed humorously apropos to this subject. Below a frazzled female cartoon character read this caption: *If you're not in a panic, you
don't understand the situation.* The same can be said of women
like us. Consider the following factors that significantly impact
a woman's material worth:

- Women own less than 1 percent of the world's property. Though we work over 60 percent of all hours worked, we only receive 10 percent of the world's income.[5]
- A poll of CEOs at Fortune 1000 companies found that over 80 percent acknowledged that discrimination impedes female employees' progress.[6]
- The average salary of an African-American female college graduate in a full-time position is less than that of a white male high school dropout.[7]
- After divorce, a woman's disposable income drops by 73 percent while a man's rises by 46 percent.[8]

Financial planner Ron Blue reports that

- seven out of twelve women will become widows;
- the average age of widows in the United States is fifty-two;
- only 2 percent of Americans ever reach the point of being able to live off the financial resources they've accumulated;
- repayment of debt consumes 25 percent of the average income today, not including mortgage debt.[9]

No wonder we worry! As the cartoon says, if we aren't in a panic, perhaps we don't understand the situation. Based on our research, most women are in a panic, at least when it's time to pay bills. The women surveyed reported financial issues as the second highest source of stress in their lives.

Financial issues resulting in stress are not usually simple problems. Money is consistently one of the four most common issues cited by couples as a source of marital tension. Many excellent books are available dealing with financial planning, household budgeting, and the powerful emotions that often surround financial issues. (See the Recommended Resources, Appendix B). To sort and simplify this complex source of stress by trying to summarize sound principles of financial planning or superficially addressing the interplay between money and emotions is beyond the scope of this book.

What we *do* want to offer is a realistic framework for women experiencing financial stress. We want to address an important "Why?"

Why do Christian women, women who have committed their lives to serving the Risen Lord, struggle with financial anxiety, concerns about the adequacy of their income, and monetary pressures? Why doesn't our relationship with Christ bring us inner peace and confidence when it comes to money? Why?

We believe that too often Christian women are framed as full of greed when in fact they are full of need. Greed is a personal spiritual issue that we can take to our Creator. He can help and will heal if we allow Him to. Need is a community reality that the body of believers must address if we wish to be faithful to our calling as Christians.

To get at the question of "why," we want to challenge you to consider two spiritually significant ways that we allow money to define our lives. We believe that one deadly impact of money among women is that we use it (1) to judge others, and (2) to judge ourselves.

JUDGING OTHERS

An old all-American myth was that if you worked hard, you would eventually succeed and your material possessions would reflect that hard work. Christians have added a new spin, embellishing the myth.

An all-American *Christian* myth is that God blesses His people by giving them material possessions. A second all-American Christian myth is that you are more spiritual if you are poor. We don't seem to be bothered by the fact that these two myths are contradictory. However, I sense a resulting tension in the body of believers from believing both.

Believing those myths, the following are also true:

- If our net worth is small, we probably have not worked hard or been productive.
- If our net worth is small, we have missed God's calling or been disobedient in some part of our life.
- If our net worth is large, we cannot appreciate the sufficiency of God in our life.
- If our net worth is large, we do not depend daily on God's provisions.

Either myth rides on a false assumption that we have the knowledge, insight, and right to evaluate other people, their life circumstances, and their worth. The statistics quoted earlier in this chapter clearly demonstrate that many factors affect women and our net worth, whether large or small. Births, deaths, divorce, and education affect how much money we do or don't have. God's financial blessings do not ride tandem with our personal work ethic.

Cultural and religious myths are not the place we need to go to put money in its place. Our Creator tells us quite clearly that money is no measure for the women and men He created (Matthew 6:25–29).

Nonetheless, money captivates our imagination. Magazines catch our eye describing the nation's wealthiest men or the Top Ten Richest Women. What's he worth? What's she worth? Even if we tell ourselves that money doesn't matter much, we're curious about those who have it.

As a Christian woman, I know I'm supposed to be immune to the magnetic pull of the green stuff. But I confess that as I toured our national Bureau of Engraving in Washington, D.C., I almost pressed my nose against the glass and drooled watching the factory line rolling out sheets of 100-dollar bills, stacking them, cutting them, binding them. The employees inspected and straightened those bills as if they were just paper! No doubt they were seeing my lifetime earnings pass through their fingers several times a week or maybe every few seconds!

When I am tempted to judge other women, to mentally categorize them on the basis of what they have or what they don't have using the dollar yardstick, I need to remember what Scripture tells us.

1. Money is temporary.

Money is an "earth" thing with no eternal value of its own. *The Wall Street Journal* recently featured a description of how Amish communities live in the United States. I could not help but compare some of my family's financial stresses with the simple life of the Amish. With all four of my children driving (with varying degrees of competence, spelled a-c-c-i-d-e-n-t-s), paychecks seem to go straight to our insurance agent's office. Our local auto repair shop knows us and our vehicles intimately. The lady who mixed the paint for our last repair and touch-up kindly told me she mixed "extra" and would save it for our next visit. (Comforting words to be sure!)

Vehicle insurance, HMOs, retirement funds, interest on charge cards, and taxes are of little concern to those communities who have chosen to live simply. Their HMO is their body of believers; their retirement umbrella is their extended family. I was reminded that money is an "earth" thing.

> Do not be overawed when a woman grows rich,
>> when the splendor of her house increases;
> for she will take nothing with her when she dies,
>> her splendor will not descend with her.
> Though while she lived she counted herself blessed—
>> and women praise you when you prosper—
> she will join the generation of her mothers,
>> who will never see the light of life.
> A woman who has riches without understanding
>> is like the beasts that perish.

Psalm 49:16–20,
with female nouns/pronouns

2. Money is a barometer.

While we do not know other women's circumstances or the reasons for how they dress, where they live, or what they do with their dollars, we can understand that those facts are between them and their Creator. Additionally, only God knows what is going on inside a person under the external facade.

When Paul talks about our human differences in Romans 14, he reminds us that we are not to judge one another. "Who are you to judge someone else's servant? To her own master she stands or falls" (Romans 14:4, with female pronouns).

Pretend for a moment. What if the story told in Mark 10 about the rich young ruler were told of a woman, not a man? What understanding could we gain from the story?

A rich young woman heard that Jesus was in the area. She ran up to him, fell on her knees, and said, "Good teacher, what must I do to inherit eternal life? I want to live forever."

He answered, "Why do you call me good? No one is good—except God alone. You know the commandments: Do not murder, do not commit adultery, do not steal, do not give false testimony, do not defraud, honor your father and mother. You know all the rules."

"Teacher," she said looking him straight in the eye, "I have followed these rules since I was a girl."

Jesus looked at her and loved her.

"You're missing something. Go sell everything you have and give to the poor, and you will have treasure in heaven. Then come, follow me."

The rich young leader's face fell. She turned and walked away sad because she had great wealth. She had stumbled at the first commandment: "Thou shalt have no other gods before me."

Onlookers on the road that day probably had a host of reactions. As the rich woman approached, some might have thought, *Now here comes someone Jesus needs—good reputation,*

*money to help with the daily cost of operations for His traveling
band. He needs to sign her on.*

When Jesus asked the rich woman to give away all she had,
Jesus was laying the barometer face up showing what she valued.
She had chosen money as her god, not Jesus. Whether her
money was in her pocket or the poor people's pockets was not
a big deal to Jesus. He was concerned with what took top priority
in her life. Money served as a barometer of her values.

Jesus used this teachable moment with His disciples to say,
"How hard it is for the rich to enter the kingdom of God!"
(Mark 10:23).

God uses all kinds of methods to remind me that money is
just a barometer. In my own life, God has used my home as His
object lesson.

We have a lovely home. Compared to my expectations as a
poor farm girl who lived in a home without running water, I live
in a mansion today. We came by it unexpectedly, through a combination of eager sellers and rare timing in the cycles of real estate. In human terms, our purchase of the house was a real estate
fluke: a buyer's dream and a seller's sigh of relief to be rid of a
headache. In God's terms, however, it was "sanctified coinci-
dence." God had a plan for that house and our home.

My husband and I loved the area in which this house is lo-
cated. We frequently drove through the neighborhoods, admir-
ing the spacious homes, stately evergreens, and mature willows.
We looked at the house on a whim knowing it was way beyond
what we could ever afford; nonetheless, one sunny afternoon the
"Open House" sign drew us magnetically to simply walk
through. The home had been vacant and on the market for
months.

"You know, this house was sold once and then rented when
the sale fell through," the realtor told us. "The owner is ready
to get rid of it. Make any offer you can—and see what happens!"

My husband and I made our unlikely offer on this home as

I rushed off to speak at a seminar. Our one-time, non-negotiable offer, the absolute maximum we could afford, was still thousands of dollars below market value and the asking price. Late that night in the motel room I lay in bed alternating between praying and fretting, first worrying that our offer would *not* be accepted, then worrying that our offer *would* be accepted. Another speaker for the seminar lay quietly snoring in the next bed. We both needed our focused energy for the next day, but I continued to mull options in my mind.

Then the words of Scripture came clearly to mind: "On the [hill] of the Lord it will be provided" (Genesis 22:14). God provided a ram in the bushes when Abraham was willing to give up Isaac.

I relished those words and the peace God gave me that night. Our offer was accepted. The seller was happy with having dependable buyers. Bob and I had the home on the hill.

Having the gift of hospitality, my husband and I somewhat hesitantly began opening our home to others, sometimes almost apologetically for the comforts we were enjoying and sharing.

On one occasion we hosted a family in our home overnight. Although I knew very little of their financial status, they revealed that they had little. This family had great peace and satisfaction and expressed that God provided for them daily. I was happy to have shared our home, thankful that we have, at this time in our lives, space to share with others.

Later, I received a photocopied article from this family about the benefits of poverty with portions highlighted. As I read the article, I was tempted to feel unspiritual and guilty for having what I consider a lovely home.

"Wait, Miriam."

The Holy Spirit, who works overtime reminding me what God has done in my life, gave me a gentle refresher lesson.

"Remember the night you prayed regarding this house on the hill?"

How well I remembered that night. Laying aside the high-lighted reminders, laying aside the fear of sharing our home lest we be judged for its abundant comforts, I thanked God for providing this house on the hill.

How many times God has laid the barometer of my heart for Him face up through this home. We now face some costly repairs, at the same time we are having to take care of other expenses I never dreamed we'd have—just as I never dreamed I'd have this home. So we're now praying for God's "healing of the toilets" with a smile, but also with honest-to-God serious faith that when He begins something, He finishes it. Not to worry.

JUDGING OURSELVES

One of the insidious barbs of the myth that God always blesses with material stuff is the other side of the coin. If I'm not rich, or at least comfortable, there's something wrong with me! Since we've put the rich guy on the pedestal, and I'm not rich, I belong in the mud.

I see women evaluate themselves based on what they have. "I'm poor; therefore I'm nobody," so the reasoning goes.

My two sisters fleshed out for me the reality of the divorce statistics cited earlier. Both suffered financially, and both tell me that, while the divorce was the greatest blow to their sense of self-worth, the follow-up financial plunge added to their struggle.

They have both over time fleshed out their belief in Paul's words:

> I know what it is to be in need, and I know what it is
> to have plenty. I have learned the secret of being content in
> any and every situation, whether well fed or hungry,
> whether living in plenty or in want.
>
> Philippians 4:12

One sister, having moved from a nine-room home to a two-

room apartment, then to being a boarder with kitchen privi-
leges, struggled to rediscover who she was. And she did. I recently admired an interesting pottery piece hanging on the wall
of her new home.

"It's from the resale shop," she responded with quiet pleasure.

Thank you, sister, for showing me real living.

My other sister offers me coffee in her new home. She
reaches for the pot, whose spot is on top of the refrigerator since
that is the only available counter space for it. Her one-room studio in a converted old painted lady home is not blessed with
cabinet space. I clear a space on her couch/bed for our tray. I
imagine her celebration in this room with her three children at
Christmas, the smell of roast and Yorkshire pudding, her spe-
cialty. Ostrich feathers in the window and assorted house plants
shout to outsiders that she is definitely still herself. Her pet fer-
ret, the Weez, shows that living things, color, and the unique
remain, though all else seems changed.

My sisters have shown me the secret of being content.

The struggle to rediscover ourselves may be equally difficult
for women who have always lived with little and then have
much. Such was the case with Rhonda.

Rhonda's identity had for years been "the pastor's wife." As
is frequently the case, they had little stuff. Early they had concluded they would always purchase their own home as they
moved from place to place in order to have a home for which
their family felt ownership. Following their usual family guidelines, they purchased their third family home, adequate for them
and their two grade school children. After seven years in the
pastorate, they prepared to accept a call to a new location. Values
of real estate had gone up dramatically, so they made a good
profit on the sale of their home, and homes in the new community were quite reasonable.

"I moved into a paid-for home, no mortgage. I could hardly

adjust. Miriam, I didn't know what it was like to shop not having to weigh every penny spent. It sounds crazy, but those were hard days."

Those words were said ten years ago. I happen to know that she is still a ferocious sales shopper and loves a good flea market. Her husband now works for a parachurch organization, and she has an acute sensitivity to the needs of pastors' wives. She has a new appreciation for these words: "Command those who are rich in this present world not to be arrogant nor to put their hope in wealth, which is so uncertain, but to put their hope in God, who richly provides us with everything for our enjoyment" (1 Timothy 6:17).

She is learning to enjoy. And the lesson has not come automatically.

When we are tempted to judge ourselves based on how much money we have or how much stuff we have, we need to ask ourselves:

- Says who? Who is telling me my worth is based on what material things I own?
- What person or people have created this reality for me? How does it serve that person? Myself?
- What would be different if I stopped believing that?

What can women do who are hooked on the belief that their value is based on what they have? We may decide in our minds that we want to change how we think. But sometimes habits die hard.

Debra and her husband attended a fortieth birthday party for a friend at an exclusive country club. Guests were invited to arrive an hour before dinner to play croquet (an optional activity), followed by an informal buffet. Debra and Gary decided to go just for the buffet because of a wedding they were to attend earlier that afternoon. When they arrived, Debra quickly realized they were not dressed in the appropriate "country club" attire: the men were wearing golf sweaters, golf shoes, and starched khakis; the women were wearing what Debra described as "casual sophisticated" attire. Wearing what they had worn to the wedding left her feeling self-conscious, overdressed, and out of place.

"Miriam, I think the thing that made me feel so out of place was knowing that even if we hadn't just come from the wedding, we *still* wouldn't have worn the *right* thing—we don't even *own* 'golfing clothes,' " Debra told me later. "As long as I allowed myself to wish I'd worn something else, I was miserable. Once I took the focus off myself and turned my attention to others, I relaxed and enjoyed myself."

Sound like adolescent insecurity? Exactly. No matter what our age, social status, or circumstances, old habits die hard. We still all too easily find ourselves comparing ourselves to others, and in the process, judging them or judging ourselves.

When Debra or I need an "attitude adjustment" we try to look at what is truly important; we try to remind ourselves of what has *real* value.

At a time when I needed to remind myself of just how wealthy I am, I began jotting down a list of some of the "things" that enrich my life. After the list in my journal reached twenty, I decided to type it up and keep it with me for those inevitable moments when I think the bank account is insufficient. Here's my list. What would you have on a list of your own?

1. Watching a beautiful sunset.
2. Overhearing my child tell a friend about something special I did.
3. Listening to beautiful music in peaceful surroundings.
4. Completing a job that I find meaningful.
5. Finally mastering a new skill after much concentration and hard work.

6. Pausing to catch my breath and relax my muscles after vigorous physical exercise.
7. Receiving a compliment on the quality of my work from my supervisor.
8. Cross-country skiing.
9. Pausing to watch a child playing in a pile of leaves on a beautiful fall day.
10. Soaking in a warm bath.
11. Lying on the ground with cool grass under my back and the warmth of the sun soaking my skin.
12. Feeling at peace with God and myself during a quiet early-morning walk.
13. Savoring a delicious meal of well-prepared food.
14. Watching someone I've mentored begin to experience success.
15. Completing a complicated task.
16. Realizing my physical fitness efforts are paying off.
17. Being able to see someone through a difficult situation when they've called on me for help during an emergency.
18. Discovering that I can talk to one of my friends about anything and I'm accepted just as I am.
19. Realizing one of my children has handled a difficult situation responsibly.
20. Watching the seeds of a thistle take off in the wind.

Now what about your list? Make your own list of the delights and pleasures of living. What are the first things that come to mind? What are the moments you feel God's presence most intimately? When do you feel great joy? You might like to read Psalm 104:1–25 quietly, slowly, before writing your list.

The delights and pleasures of living

_____

_____

_____

_____

_____

_____

_____

_____

_____

_____

_____

_____

_____

As I read what David wrote in Psalm 104, I'm reminded that our Creator has given us an incredible planet to enjoy, no admission required, no cover charge necessary.

What are we worth? We may not be included on the ten richest women list, but we are worth more to our Creator than a mountain dancing with wild flowers that He created just for the sheer pleasure of their vibrant delicate beauty.

NOTES

1. William J. Bennett, *The Index of Leading Cultural Indicators*, Vol. I (published jointly by Empower America, The Heritage Foundation, Free Congress Foundation, March 1993), p. 9.
2. *An American Profile: Opinions and Behavior 1972–89* (Gale Research).
3. Bennett, op. cit., p. 9.
4. Harriet Meyer, "Fighting the Teen-Pregnancy War," *Chicago Tribune*, (16 Aug. 1994).
5. Steven Myers, "Crown of Beauty Instead of Ashes," *World Christian Summer Reader*, 20–25 (Pasadena, Calif.: World Christian, 1990), p. 22.
6. Swain and Swain, *Statistics, International Institute of Speakers and Speechwriters*, cited in *Enterprise* (Southwestern Bell), p. 6.
7. *The Facts About Women* (New York: Women's Action Coalition, The New Press, 1993), p. 59.
8. Ibid, pp. 59- 60.
9. Ron Blue, *Master Your Money Workbook* (Nashville: Thomas Nelson, 1993), p. 9; sources for statistics quoted by Ron Blue include the Social Security Board, Devney's Economic Tables, and the Department of Commerce.

Five

The Perfect Christian Wife
and Other Elusive Dreams

D*ebra speaks:*
"George, have you met Debbie, the pastor's wife?" came the question from behind a pleasant smile.

GRRRRRRRRR. I hate being introduced as "the pastor's wife." The pastor's wife. I shudder when I hear the phrase. I vowed to myself in college I would never marry a minister; I just couldn't see myself in that role. God had other plans. Nonetheless, those three simple words conjure up images of a colorless, lifeless, frumpy woman wearing a prim little jumper, high-buttoned blouse, with shapeless hair and no makeup. A doting mother, dutiful wife, and soft-spoken woman. Sweet, demure, submissive. In short, everything I'm not. The only thing worse is being introduced as "our pastor's wife." *Our* pastor's wife? Does answering a call include right of ownership? I always wonder where the bill of sale is kept.

"Hi! I'm Debra Klingsporn," I say warmly, putting as much emphasis on Debra as I can get away with while extending my hand and minding my manners. "It's so nice to meet you."

Debra. The name is Debra, not Debbie.

Debbie is a nickname I left behind years ago along with considerable emotional baggage. When someone calls me Debbie, I'm thrust into an emotional time warp of adolescent insecurities. Suddenly I'm twenty pounds heavier, reaching for the Clearasil, fighting bad hair days on a daily basis, and looking for a hole in the ground I can disappear into.

"Her name is *Debra*," asserts my eight-year-old daughter, "not Debbie." I sheepishly smile, laugh, and think, *Why can't I say that?* My daughter has an easier time with assertiveness than I do.

With my husband on the staff of a large suburban church, you'd think I'd get over what I call the "cringe impact" of that innocuous little phrase. But after fifteen years of marriage and ministry, I still haven't. I doubt I ever will. When I hear, "This is Debbie, our pastor's wife," I still cringe. I still want to snarl, growl, or worse.

The problem is not with the phrase. Many talented women are named Debbie; many women proudly wear the mantle of "pastor's wife." No, the cringe impact is not a matter of semantics. The problem is with the roles, stereotypes, and expectations I associate with those simple little innocent words.

Roles. Stereotypes. Expectations. We all have them. We all live with them. We are both recipients and purveyors of their impact. Casual conversation and everyday occurrences easily land us in the cringe-impact zone of women's roles.

For example, few women I know can remain emotionally indifferent when meeting parents of their children's schoolmates for the first time, and the question arises, "Do you work outside the home?" (Translation: Do you have a life?) Either way, whether you work outside the home or stay home with your kids, most women I know hate that question. No matter which choice we're living, for most of us some degree of guilt (cringe) accompanies our response to that simple query.

Or consider how easily we fall into the cringe-impact zone: your boss moves a deadline up and you've made a commitment to your family. Do you (cringe) say no to your boss—or (cringe) renege on your family?

Our lives as women are significantly shaped, molded, and defined by the roles, expectations, and stereotypes we carry around inside our heads, coloring our thinking with shades of *ought to*'s, *should do*'s, and *have to*'s. The line between what's right and what's wrong, what's important and what's trivial, what's necessary and what's superfluous is often difficult to distinguish. When we add to the mix the desire to be successful, the pressure we feel is even greater.

I'm at times amused, at times amazed, at the preconceived ideas others have about me once they learn that I'm married to a minister.

"Oh, I think it's so great that you are staying home with your children. I just don't understand these women that think they have to be out there doing it all when the most important thing they can do is raise their kids." Yes, but I *work* at home, not just casually, not just occasionally. I don't bake cookies. I don't cook well-balanced meals every night or greet my daughters at the door after school with made-from-scratch healthy snacks. (We eat Cheerios for supper more often than I care to confess, and my kids think French fries from McDonald's are a household staple.)

"You? You're a pastor's wife?! But, but, you're so, you know, you're so normal!" As if most pastors' wives aren't normal?

"You're Pastor Klingsporn's wife, aren't you? Well, would you tell him to call me about the. . . ." Ahhh, yes, the dutiful pastor's wife always provides live-in secretarial services.

"Well, you're pretty conservative, aren't you? Your husband is a minister, isn't he?" Hmmm. Conservative. Now there's a word full of assumptions and stereotypes. Let's see, does that mean conservative fiscally, politically, or theologically?

Labels. Assumptions. Preconceived ideas we bring to the table aren't limited to pastors' wives and dinner-party conversations. Miriam, too, has come up against the expectations for the "perfect Christian wife."

LEARNING THE DO'S AND DON'TS THE HARD WAY

Miriam speaks:

I remember one of my first lessons on "the look." I was at a lakeside gathering for families in my husband's company. I had always worn a two-piece swimsuit when we took our kids to the lake or pool. Without giving any thought to my choice of swimsuit I wore my two-piece while we were attending the conference. My baby daughter and I were enjoying the sand and sun while my husband was in meetings. Unexpectedly, a gentleman approached me and asked me how many minutes I would need to change my attire. No explanation, no request.

I was puzzled and embarrassed, but more hurt than anything else. Not having been raised in a religiously restrictive home, I was caught totally off guard by the conservative code of dress. I realized afterward that I was expected to know and share an unspoken, yet clearly defined set of criteria for appropriate appearance and behavior. Whether spoken or unspoken, acknowledged or denied, we all have an image of the "successful" Christian mother and wife. All too often our definition of success for Christian women is determined by what our husband has accomplished and the level of achievement of our children—by secular standards. Education, income, athletic ability, even appearance count.

How are we aware of the image? During the Christmas season, spread the Christmas letters you receive across your kitchen table. What news do we share? Look at the front covers of Christian magazines, look at the photographs in your children's Sunday school handouts and advertisements for literature supporting "family values." Christian families have "a look." Christian women have an image. And whether we know it or not, the hierarchy of God, husband, children, church, (and on the bottom rung) work, and self have had an unmistakable impact on Christian women today, particularly when we don't fit the cookie-cutter formula.

WHAT'S AT THE CENTER OF OUR ORBIT?

In this past year one of my dearest lifelong friends, a woman I have always admired for her intelligence and insight, came to the recognition that she idolized her marriage. She had put her husband on a pedestal; their marriage became a god in her life. Her insight struck a chord of recognition in my own soul.

For many women, it is as though our husband becomes the sun in our universe, our children become the planets circling the sun, and we, "the good mothers," try to be moons keeping in sync with a path around each child that must be circled at a prescribed pace—or the universe will reel into disorder. Many a harried Christian wife and mother says, "Yes. That describes my world. I know the feeling. I'm peddling as fast as I can. And someone else set the pace of the treadmill. It wasn't me! I would never create this dither for myself."

Did God do it?

Would a loving God have this in mind when He created male and female? He formed the first institution of marriage and created this thing called family. Is this how He meant it to be?

I think not. Logic tells us that the God who, in love, created people would not create an institution that would destroy women or contradict His original creation: two people in His image, created to worship Him, not each other, nor the institution He created.

We've heard tons about the demise of the American family. We have volumes written by Christians about what's wrong with the American family, why the divorce rate has climbed, why children are neglected. It is easy to blame those worldly outside forces for destroying our families.

It's easy to point the finger at those terrible outside forces that creep into Christian marriages and create havoc.

May I offer a different perspective? Many Christian marriages and families have been destroyed from within as much or even more than by those outside forces. A "Christian Family" mold has been created. And many committed Christian women who love God don't fit the "perfect Christian family" mold. I see authentic Christian women being tempted to blame God for the misfit rather than rejecting the mold and refusing to give the mold makers license to create those molds.

In Christian circles it is popular to decry feminist thinking that drives women to hate men, materialism that woos women out into the workplace to the neglect of their families, and self-ishness that makes them think of their own needs rather than others. These popular cries rouse Christians to rise up and defend a diseased institution that will continue to die due to internal causes, regardless of how much "protection" Christian marriages are offered from outside attacks.

Christian women have been encouraged to idolize their marriages. We have been encouraged to idolize our families. Idols in good standing for the Christian woman in the Christian community and the Christian church are her husband and her children. It is not only accepted but often expected that a Christian woman offer her body, soul, mind, and spirit at the altar of her family. According to the "perfect Christian family" mold, we are more "spiritual" if we neglect our needs and gifts, putting the needs and desires of our husbands and families first. "Good" Christian wives and moms have been encouraged to neglect their own physical, emotional, and mental health for their families.

As a young mother I remember hearing a Mother's Day sermon built around the story of a prairie hen. A fire sweeps across the plains. Mother hen calls her chicks to her, they huddle under her wings, and the fire descends on them. The grass quickly burns and the wind sweeps the wall of flames on. The carcass of the mother, crisped in death, moves gently. More movement. The chicks have been saved. They scamper out alive. The wonderful mother hen has sacrificed herself for her children.

What happens to the chicks? My guess is that foxes and hawks or weasels and wolves discover an easy lunch.

When I see my black sisters pictured weeping on the front of our Chicago newspapers over the shooting deaths of their children, I think of this graphic picture of the sacrificial prairie hen. Women alone in many families, especially in our black communities, are trying to protect their children. Statistics show us that it is not working. And it certainly was never God's intention that a mother hold both ends of the hammock called family.

Nancy Beech at Willow Creek Community Church thankfully did not give the prairie hen illustration in her Mother's Day message. She offered a better model. Every time you fly, before the plane leaves the ground, you hear the safety speech: "If you have small children, when the oxygen masks drop down, secure the mask over your face and then assist your child."

Does this sound cruel? Not at all. We know that if we cannot survive, we cannot offer our children the oxygen they will need. Some Christian wives feel they are responsible for putting oxygen masks on their husbands first. It's being a "good wife." A man's apparent need must come first, even though she joins the kamikaze ranks in order to meet or match his agenda. If this strikes no chord of recognition in you, feel free to skip the rest of this chapter! For those of you who feel a tickle of truth in that illustration, read on.

Bev approached me at a conference to tell me her story. She was struggling with the gender thing. She disliked men. She was a growing Christian and felt compelled to come to peace with all people—men included. Prompted by a few questions, it became obvious that Bev had done some good mind and feeling work discovering insights into the roots of her "do I want to connect or disconnect" feeling about men.

She had looked at what she learned about men from her mother. Bev's mother felt contempt for men. She had been one of twelve children, nine of whom were girls, and all felt contempt for men. This dramatic pattern did not materialize without cause. Bev's grandmother had borne and raised all these children, supported them by her work, while her husband remained unemployed most of his life.

"She was willing to work herself to death and he was willing to let her," Bev's mother had said about her mother.

Bev's anger became obvious; she carried her mother's baton of contempt. "And Grandma's tombstone reads, *She Never Thought of Herself.*" This out-of-balance family hammock was swinging the third-generation women wild.

While the life-style of Bev's grandmother and grandfather may have been extreme and unique, the message on the tombstone is not. God told men and women to subdue the earth and populate it together (Genesis 1:28). When they tripped up and decided to follow their own agenda, those two tasks were never done together—in harmony—again (Genesis 3). Men=work, women=family is the divided message sent in traditional Christian circles in the United States today. Mutuality—shared subduing and multiplying—is hard to find.

As I look at other countries, the world picture is just as devoid of mutuality, though perhaps with less expectation of united men and women.

As we reported in Chapter 4, women own less than 1 percent of the world's property; though they work over 60 percent of all hours worked, they only receive 10 percent of the world's income.[1] Genesis 1:26 says, "Let us make man [and woman] in our image, in our likeness, and let them rule over the fish of the sea and the birds of the air, over the livestock, over all the earth, and over all the creatures that move along the ground." Matthew 10:10 reads, "A workman or woman is worthy of her wages" (author's paraphrase). In light of these two verses, this imbalance is certainly not what God intended. Yet when we allow this imbalance to remain the model in our marriages, we are condoning an injustice affecting half of God's creation—the female half.

MOVING TOWARD MUTUAL MARRIAGES: WHAT HELPS, WHAT HINDERS

Through different decades in our history, the imbalance has swung one way and then another. Currently, in some Christian circles, women can be employed, under prescribed conditions and with defined relationships, excluding any authority or leadership over men. In some Christian organizations, men can't participate in family and be as devoted to family matters without a cloud gathering over their professional commitment. If men adapt their lives too much to family needs, the organization wonders if they have it all under control, as a "spiritual" man should.

Indicators in the general population show that some men may be staying home as "housedads" while their wives pursue a career. In some Christian circles this is simply not the right and proper order. Christian women may have more freedom than men to try to do it all. Fortunately this is not typical in all Christian communities, but the fact that it continues to be true in many is cause for concern.

My research shows that married women do the greatest amount of household tasks even when they are employed outside the home. How can Christian women be employed and do most of the household tasks? Only by living the message on the tombstone: *She Never Thought of Herself.*

That tombstone inscription explains a disease that causes

stress at best and can cause serious illness in Christian marriage. More than half (55 percent) of Christian women work full-time. Another 15 percent work part-time. When there are children in the home, women do 80 percent of the tasks related to the children and 70 percent of the tasks related to the home. Mutual sharing of the tasks of survival and relationship is still a dream in most Christian marriages, not a reality.

DOES IT WORK?

What happens to real Christian women in real marriages with real kids when this is the accepted, expected life-style?

I participate in a small study group with several other Christian women. As we clustered around the table with our coffee cups in hand, we wrestled with this issue of mutuality and the reality that most women "do it all" when it comes to keeping a household running. One member of the group expressed what many women, including Christian women, feel: "I'm sick and tired of being sick and tired."

Each of us commiserated about the feeling that we were usually running on our last ounce of energy, that if anything went askew in our juggling act, we would not have the strength to extend our arms one more quarter of an inch to catch whatever piece of our lives or our families was falling.

We dug beneath the surface stuff. How did we feel about God? What priority was He in our lives?

We all felt that God was keenly aware of our struggles and in loving compassion felt for the burdens we carried.

We read Scripture about His love. We read Scripture about marriage. We looked up words in our concordances and dug for truth. Our conclusion with our open Bibles and study bathed in prayer was that God's good intention was not that our marriages be so lopsided.

More than once in our study group, we found ourselves looking at the stress points of our marriages and recognizing stress points for what they were—a result of the virus in Christian marriage that not only allows but encourages imbalance between husband and wife.

Most of us in our study group married "good men." For most of us, neither spouse in the marriage knowingly chose the lopsided restrictions of the Christian culture. We just walked in blindly believing we would live happily ever after because we both loved God.

In order to survive the imbalance in marriage in today's Christian culture, many women have had to go through mental gymnastics to rationalize what is happening in their real lives.

Some have come to the conclusion that the person they see in the mirror, the woman God created, is not as important to the man they married as they dream and wish she were.

Repeatedly we arrive at stress points. Some women just hear their body of believers saying "submit." "He's the authority, that's the way it is supposed to work. What's wrong with your willingness, woman? Did you not expect that following Christ would require sacrifice?" (And we remember the prairie hen story.)

Then when we hear a message via sermon or seminar that we are special, we wonder what that really means. Do we count as much? Does "special" mean that we are ordained to handle all the midnight feedings, change 80 percent of the dirty diapers, and clean the toilets eight out of ten times? Or does "mutual" apply to all of those tasks and countless more? Does "mutual" apply when we need companionship during the week of the football, basketball, or baseball playoffs? (Pity the woman whose husband is a fan of all three!)

"Mutual" goes well beyond the "big" decisions—where to live, or whether or not to make a job change. Mutual applies to everything as mundane as laundry and grocery shopping, shuttling kids to baseball practice and doctor's appointments. Mutual means just that—mutually sharing the load.

If there are stress points in a marriage, it is sometimes assumed that the wife should receive counseling to take care of her problems, to become strong enough to submit better, to bear her burdens more silently. The women in our study group could not remember leaders, mentors, pastors, or teachers who discouraged them from idolizing the man they married or the institution itself. They were rarely challenged and pointed directly to God.

"Mutual?"

"Leave and cleave" as a principle for wives *and* husbands?

Our Christian communities need to get back to looking at the bare Word for our model, rather than the words of human mold makers.

GOD HAS AN EXCELLENT PLAN

Our study group discovered that God cares and that we matter to Him. Imbalance in marriage or idolizing our husbands is not, and never was, God's idea. It is human beings who have chosen to live continually with this imbalance—and because of the assumed superiority of the husband's position in a marriage, we continue to give priority to his desires and needs over the needs of all other family members.

When we spend a lifetime giving deference to another human being, it is difficult not to make that person—or the institution of marriage itself—an idol. But the first commandment of my Creator is that I have no gods before Him. And it is my intention and my heart's greatest passion to be obedient to Him.

How can Christian women today avoid the trap of idolizing marriage or the man they married? We can begin by asking ourselves questions and looking at the direction we're going.

GOD'S EXCELLENT PLAN: MUTUALITY BETWEEN WIVES AND HUSBANDS

How do we assess whether we are moving toward mutuality or living in the trap of idolizing our marriage? Ask yourself a few hard questions. Perhaps journal and pray about these questions for a few days, then talk over your reflections with a trusted (and honest) friend.

- Are decisions that affect both of us made with deference to one person?
- Is preference given to the needs of one over another on a habitual basis?
- Is one God-created person habitually diminished for the sake of the relationship?
- Is the admonition to "submit to *one another* out of reverence for Christ" (Ephesians 5:21) instruction that guides our marriage?
- Is love practiced through servanthood the standard for *both* of us in our marriage?

Many women can sense when the relationship is becoming an idol, when things are lopsided and you feel more like a workhorse than a wife. Rather than ignore the feeling, we encourage you to look carefully at your marriage. Examine your heart, your spirit, your feelings, and trust what you hear in your thoughts during quiet moments. You and I know it's hard to move toward balance in an unbalanced marriage. Initiating change is like swallowing bad-tasting medicine. But considering the alternatives (divorce statistics in the Christian community match general statistics), it's worth the effort. It is easier to chart a mutual course early in a relationship than change directions after stubborn habits have encrusted two people in an idol trap.

When a marriage is ailing or sick, even though nobody has noticed or is loudly complaining, it is never wise to leave the virus undisturbed. We need rather to expose that virus to the truth of God's Word and let God show us the way to a healthier relationship.

Our motivation to follow God's guidelines in any relationship is to be obedient to God. However, in the case of Christian marriage, there is another worthwhile, secondary motivation. Our example to people who do not personally know our Creator is vital today. Healthy marriages in the body of believers would be a definite beacon light in these United States.

MARRIAGE ASSESSMENT: WHO DECIDES AND HOW?

My husband and I have talked about important, life-shaping choices and discovered that most major decisions have been made—not by discussion and mutual agreement—but by assumption and default. Because we have a tenacious commitment to each other and to a mutual marriage relationship, we continually take the risk of asking whether this is how we *want* things to be. We have found eight decision-making issues that are key issues for most married couples. Whether you're a newlywed or living well past your first decade as a married person, we encourage you to review the following important topics.

A helpful exercise is to review this list independently of each other; then compare your responses. Some of these issues may open emotional discussions; if you find the discussion with your spouse laced with anger and resentment, don't back away from the issue or "table it" indefinitely. Acknowledge that you've "hit a nerve" and agree to a method of talking through the difficulty.[2]

1. Where do we live and how do we decide? (Near family or far away from relatives? Which state or country? In the city, a suburb, or out in the country? Was/is the decision based on a job or other factors?)

2. What criteria do we use to choose where we live? (How much mortgage do we take on? What size/kind of house? How much of our discretionary income goes to housing?)

3. What about family (having children or choosing not to, deciding when our family is complete, who does most of the "active" parenting, i.e., discipline, decision making, etc.)

4. Tasks of family living:

- Home (inside versus outside tasks; maintenance and repair versus day-to-day clutter control and routine cleaning)
- Vehicles (Who decides what kind of car, how much to spend, when to buy a new one? Who takes care of maintenance?)
- Meals and eating (including shopping and cleanup)

5. Employment:

- Who is able to do what?
- Whose abilities are used in the marketplace?
- Are the choices mutually satisfying to both spouses?

6. Children:

- Whose schedule flexes to care for the children?
- Who visits the school and attends conferences?
- Who volunteers in the school?
- Who does what tasks?

7. Vacations:

- Whose hobbies and activities influence area and activities?
- What portion of income goes for vacations?

8. Holidays:

- Which family of origin will be dominant?
- What new traditions would we like for our marriage?

Save your notes. You will, no doubt, find it a growing experience to look back on them later.

IS IT TOO LATE TO CHANGE?

If you did not talk about these things before marriage (and most of us don't), join the large crowd of women—including myself—who have muddled through after the fact and are still in process. It's never too late to explore changing the level of mutuality in your marriage. The following questions may provide a litmus test of how you feel about your relationship:

- Can either you or your husband express satisfaction or dissatisfaction with your physical relationship?
- Can either you or your husband express stress points in your marriage (regarding children, your life-style, or finances, to name a few)?
- What level of discomfort has to be reached before a stress point is discussed?
- Do you come to mutual resolutions? (i.e., Can you *both* say, "We reached this conclusion together"?)
- Does your decision-making process as a couple reflect the equal worth of both of you?

In Jesus' day a common sight was a donkey carrying supplies along the dusty roads of Judea. Some were so loaded down you could hardly see them beneath their burdens. If you could visualize you and your mate as a pair, visualize your burdens. Are they mutually carried? Is one more engulfed in her or his stuff and the stuff of marriage?

While it may be painful to recognize inequity initially, long-range health in any relationship depends on it.

When I assess my marriage, I ask trusted friends to help me see myself and check my thinking. I will always remember one wise woman's advice: "Be careful whose counsel you seek."

I needed to hear her words. I was comforted by her concern for my personal welfare, laying aside the surface issues of my position, my husband's image, etc. She advised me to talk to those who believe God is equally as concerned for me as a *person* (not just a wife) as He is for my husband. She was wise, for the circles we sometimes draw about ourselves often limit our sources of support and wisdom.

GOD'S EXCELLENT PLAN: JESUS IS OUR HIGH PRIEST

There is a teaching in some Christian circles that the husband functions as a high priest in his family. Such a hierarchy within marriage has no basis in Scripture. The Scriptures are clear about the priesthood of ALL believers (1 Peter 2:9). Since the curtain to the Holy of Holies was ripped from top to bottom the day that Golgotha wept, each Christian enters God's presence and speaks to Him directly.

To study this more thoroughly, consider the following Scripture passages:

> But you are a chosen race, a royal priesthood, a holy nation, God's own people in order that you may proclaim the mighty acts of him who called you out of darkness into his marvelous light.
>
> 1 Peter 2:9, NRSV

Note that "you" is the generic term for all believers.

> Then each one will receive commendation from God.
>
> 1 Corinthians 4:5, NRSV

This verse refers to when we will each stand before God as individuals at the time of judgment. (Note "each one.")

> I appeal to you therefore, brothers and sisters, by the mercies of God, to present your bodies as a living sacrifice, holy and acceptable to God which is your spiritual worship.
>
> Romans 12:1, NRSV

Note that each presents herself or himself; no person offers another.

I can promise you a rich, rich time of study if you dig deeper into Scripture on your position directly connected to our God with Jesus alone providing that access. It does not surprise me that the teaching of the husband functioning as a high priest in a family has crept into the church. It is an age-old tactic of the evil one to convince believers that someone stands between them and God. Martin Luther fought this deception with the Roman Catholic church. Most cult leaders begin by wedging themselves between people and God.

Fortunately, women can hold this teaching up to the light of Scripture. It does not pass the scrutiny for truth. "You shall have no other gods before me" (Exodus 20:3).

REDISCOVERING MARRIAGE BETWEEN CHRISTIANS

Debra speaks:

The survey findings confirm what most of us know from experience. In most marriages, *especially* Christian marriages, women do most of the work. Is mutuality really possible? Is it possible to "bear one another's burdens" without Christian women feeling like the beasts of burden?

Are you reading this chapter, rolling your eyes, inwardly groaning, and thinking, "Okay, I do the laundry, buy the groceries, cook the meals, clean the house, and get the kids to practices, appointments, and lessons. I write the thank-you notes, send the Christmas cards, and buy the kids' clothes. Women do most of the work? So tell me something I don't already know!

"And now I'm supposed to sit down with my husband, talk through all this, point out to him that it's not fair, and (really pulling in the big guns) also inform him that it's not *biblical!* Then things are going to miraculously change and he's going to start scrubbing toilets and folding clothes? I don't think so!"

I know that feeling! I also know the hopelessness of feeling like "things will never change."

For the first six years of our marriage, Gary was in graduate school and I was the income earner. I was the one who lived the corporate mentality, intent on a career in publishing. Gary taught classes as a teaching assistant, did freelance writing, and worked on his dissertation. His was the "flex" schedule: he bought groceries, kept the house picked up, did the dishes, and made the undesirable trips to the laundromat. The mutuality in our relationship was enviable.

That was *before* kids. Then things changed. While on maternity leave, I quickly realized breast-feeding makes "mutuality" impossible when it comes to night feedings—and since most babies' bodily functions *always* occur simultaneously with feedings, I quickly took the lead in the tally count on changing dirty diapers.

Initially that was okay; we were mutually in agreement that we wanted to have a family and only the female body is equipped for certain tasks. Unfortunately, patterns once begun become very difficult to change. Mom as "parent on call" became firmly established. The exhaustion of that first year of motherhood caught me completely by surprise.

But then came an even *bigger* change. Gary accepted a call to a church 1,500 miles away from family, career contacts (mine), and friends. We moved from Texas to Minnesota. Within four months I went from vice president of public relations for a national firm to a stay-at-home mom—and (to make it worse) a *pastor's wife.* Arrrrgh!!!

Our first year in Minnesota was filled with transitions. Gary was working typical "ministry" hours: early-morning breakfasts, office hours all day, all-too-frequent night meetings. Not only did mutuality go out the window, so did simple presence. He was never home, and when he was home physically, he wasn't emotionally or mentally. I was *always* home—with a toddler and another baby on the way. I found myself thinking more than once, *Women willingly do this?*

What I'm describing isn't unique to couples in ministry. The same dynamic can happen in any career path, from medicine

and law to construction or retail. A wife often hits the peak iso-
lation of the all-consuming young family stage at the same time
her husband is full tilt into career building. Needless to say, we
went through some difficult adjustments.

However, with Gary in ministry, I found it more difficult to
confront the issues. How can you tell someone he needs to
spend more time at home (or at least take out the garbage) when
the thing that takes him away is "God's work"? Taking a child
to a routine doctor's appointment doesn't seem nearly as critical
as sitting with a family whose loved one is in surgery—or so it
seemed. I ended up feeling like God and I were on opposing
teams.

Gary and I didn't begin our marriage with traditional roles.
We didn't come into the parenting years with a clearly defined
distinction that my role was in the home, his was outside the
home. We never assumed I would handle the domestic duties
and he would pursue the career. Quite the contrary. But the traditional patterns crept in and the roles evolved by default, until
I was angry, exhausted, and resentful.

That was us then. This is us now: Gary does all the grocery
shopping (even clipping coupons); he does most of the laundry;
he frequently runs "shuttle duty" getting our daughters to and
from their many activities. He even picked up *all* the cookies for
our daughter's Girl Scout troop cookie sales while I was working
to meet an important deadline. When it comes to raising daughters, he's done everything but learn how to braid hair.

You get the idea. Mutuality reigns. What happened? How did
we get from there to here? By doing exactly what Miriam has
described: working through countless difficult, and sometimes
painful, marital discussions.

Going into the specifics of how we addressed problem solving, conflict resolution, and negotiating who handles what is beyond the scope of this book. What Miriam and I hope to do is
encourage readers to question the status quo. The survey results

clearly reveal that most women feel they carry the load when it comes to child care, parenting, and running a household. Contrary to what many Christian leaders would have us believe, this division of labor is not a biblical mandate; rather, for many couples it is an outdated, culturally imposed model.

But let's face it—husbands aren't going to initiate these discussions. After all, they're the ones who walk into a home with dinner ready, open their dresser drawers to find clean underwear, and don't have a clue what it is *exactly* that moms do all day. If the woman is the beast of burden, the impetus for change has to come from the one carrying the load.

Our discussions didn't start out calmly, deliberately, and rationally. Ours were prompted by four bags of garbage by the backdoor, a snow-packed driveway, and an empty gas gauge in the car. In other words, the triggers were insignificant; the issues were monumental.

Changing patterns of behavior is never easy, but it *is* possible. Gary and I had to learn to set boundaries, both for work and parenting. We had to learn to talk through expectations and clearly state our needs. We had to be intentional about changing certain behaviors. None of those changes was easy for either one of us, but the results were worth the effort.

> So God created humankind in his image, in the image of God he created them; male and female he created them. God blessed them . . .
>
> Genesis 1:27–28, NRSV

When a marriage is based on mutuality, both male *and* female are blessed. The plan is a good one. Is it working for you?

What Do Christian Marriages Look Like?

Miriam speaks:

We've talked about what Christian marriage *isn't.* Christian

marriage isn't a cookie-cutter definition of roles and responsibilities. But if Christian marriage isn't *necessarily* the traditional
"Ozzie and Harriet" dualism, what *is* Christian marriage? How
do Christians who marry live together in mutuality, make decisions, and build a family life? Both love God, both are called
according to God's purposes. What *do* Christian marriages look
like? We feel that Christian marriage, based on mutuality, reflects four key characteristics:

1. Each Marriage Will Be Different.

God creates each person with that woman's or man's unique
fingerprint. To unite two unique people and conform them to a
cookie-cutter marriage mold doesn't make sense. The current
Christian mania for reducing faith to formulas, a lifetime of living to a seminar-shaped recipe, simply defies God being Creator
of each individual. We forget that institutions such as marriage
were made for the benefit of people, not the other way around.

Let God be creatively God.

2. An Equal Marriage Will Mirror the Nature of God.

Equality of each woman and man in marriage is not a new
idea to be credited to feminists. Equal treatment for women (or
for any people) is not an ideal borrowed from the world. Subordination is the idea practiced in the world, often brutally.
Christians have borrowed subordination of women from the
world. Wherever Christianity flourishes, people live more freely.
God is the originator of equality of men and women. Marriages
like those of Abraham and Sarah or Priscilla and Aquila were
unique in their culture in both respect and communication.
Jesus fleshed out God's principle of equality. He elevated
women. God's idea of equality in marriage was radical, *is* radical,
and flies in the face of humans' magnetic pull to subordinate
women.

Subordination of women in marriage in the United States today indicates the decline of Christianity rather than the mark of a Christian culture.

I fear that our culture today has a difficult time seeing the nature of God in relationships when it looks at Christian marriages infected with the virus of inequality.

"You are the salt of the earth. But if the salt loses its saltiness, how can it be made salty again?" (Matthew 5:13).

3. Marriage Will Honor God's Unique Imprint on Each Person.

When Jesus answered the Pharisees' question about paying taxes, He spoke to a more important issue than money. Looking at the portrait on the denarius, He asked, "Whose portrait is this? And whose inscription?"

"Caesar's," they replied.

"Give to Caesar what is Caesar's and to God what is God's."

I have God's imprint on me. Each woman has God's imprint on her. A godly marriage will not annihilate one person's God-given imprint.

4. *Marriages change as women, men, and children move through seasons.*

Each season brings a new opportunity to talk, pray, and commit ourselves again first to God's call as His creations, and then to the marriage. Our relationship with God outlasts marriage.

A simple, easy sketch of a one-size-fits-all Christian marriage does not exist. In today's hurried life-style, there is supposed to be a quick answer to everything—one minute, preferably. Alas, this is not a one-minute problem with a one-minute fix.

There are clear answers in Scripture, such as,

You shall have no other gods before me.

Exodus 20:3

"We must obey God rather than [people]!"

Acts 5:29

So then, each of us will give an account of [himself/herself] to God.

Romans 14:12

GOD'S EXCELLENT PLAN: HE WILL HELP US

You have probably read and heard lots of dismal predictions about marriage. I certainly have. However, the last word is yet to be heard.

In my research, the overwhelming majority of women (97 percent) responded that their current relationship with God is "very important to me now." Each woman can depend on God's promise to answer her questions, give her insight, and help her live in His image. The women in our survey are doing what Peter urged believers to do two thousand years ago: "So keep a firm grip on the faith" (1 Peter 5:9, The Message).

> It won't be long before this generous God who has great plans for us in Christ—eternal and glorious plans they are!—will have you put together and on your feet for good. He gets the last word: yes, He does.
>
> 1 Peter 5:10, The Message

Committed women plus God with good plans. He'll have the last word. Thank God.

NOTES

1. Steven Myers, "Crown of Beauty Instead of Ashes," *World Christian Summer Reader*, 20–25 (Pasadena, Calif.: World Christian, 1990), p. 22.
2. We encourage couples experiencing difficulty resolving conflicts in any of these areas to seek professional Christian counseling. Pastors are an excellent resource for referrals to trustworthy counselors.

Six

Mentoring:
Reshaping the Assumptions of a Younger Generation

*M*iriam speaks:

Our field-trip bus bounced along an under-construction city street. My students, Las Chicas de Hoy (The Girls of Today—they named themselves), did what kids have done for decades on buses. They sang with gusto—on key, off key, and mostly loud.

Whatta man, whatta man.

What is it about a bus that inspires singing? If they could only be this enthusiastic about writing English term papers! The lyrics of the song they sang described the anatomy of this "whatta man" awesome male they loved. These girls didn't miss a word as they sang about what their man did when they were together that made them feel so good.

They looked so carefree. Youth: so many paths ahead from which to choose. We were expanding horizons, visiting college campuses, listening to women of diversity using their gifts and leadership skills. We listened to our city treasurer, Miriam Santos, a Hispanic female who oversees $40–60 billion dollars annually in city funds. I hoped the girls were raising the bar of their aspirations, their dreams, the woman in the mirror they might become.

He's so crazy.

I wanna have his baby.

Las Chicas de Hoy created a television newscast, listened to women entrepreneurs who owned their own stores, business-women who purchased internationally and risked guessing the market for jewelry, clothing, and accessories. They listened, learned from, and questioned teachers, doctors, and social workers, all women who had achieved.

I was mentoring and molding these teen girls to maximize their full potential. The bus was their vehicle to broader hori-zons as well as their American bandstand, their moving musical platform.

He's so crazy.

I wanna have his baby.

This time I HEARD what they sang. They were singing with energy beyond what they invest in homework.

I'm too late! The words sent a shock of recognition through me. Their minds have already been programmed! As I began to resent the entertainment industry for what they are doing to "my" girls' minds, I remembered a song I used to sing on bus trips. Paul Anka crooned something to this effect: "She's thinkin' about me, she's gonna have my baby."

Men buy chocolates or flowers for women when they think of them. Small investment. Women balloon up forty pounds, expel a squiggling, bowling-ball-size, life-changing/depleting baby because we thought of a guy? In another of my old favor-ites, a girl sees her heartthrob come to the party with another girl. Her life is over; she lost her boyfriend to another girl. But wait. He dumps the other woman. She has a life again.

It's my party, and I'll cry if I want to.

We bounced to band contests and our minds were not on

John Philip Sousa. The heroine of our song inspired our passion. The girl's life is over because she lost her boyfriend to another girl. But then, miracle of miracles, the boy drops that girl and chooses our weeping star. No doubt, wedding bells are next.

Has anything really changed? I dream of making a difference for girls so they can choose. I want to offer them a legacy of freedom to choose with wisdom, to become all that they can be.

They hear my voice, and the voices of role models I bring to them. They also hear radical feminist voices: "What do you want, a man or a life?" They hear a chorus of different messages that rarely harmonize.

Some of them—unfortunately, at least 40 percent of them—will be pregnant while unmarried before they are twenty. Choosing a man will change their life.

If they choose to stay pregnant and have their baby (which most Christians agree is choosing life), their education, their career options, their decisions about marriage will be different. And statistically, measurably, the quality of their life and the child's they bear will go down. Teen child-rearing is debilitating, destabilizing, and expensive. The American economy no longer forgives such mistakes.

If they choose not to have the baby, if they choose abortion, their life is still permanently affected, not in as obvious and measurable ways, but nevertheless changed.

Has anything really changed? Do my girls of today really have more choices for their tomorrow? Does being a Christian make any difference?

Our big yellow school bus was the womb of my questions. But as is frequent in my life, I had no time to ponder and sort these questions to my satisfaction.

"Can we skip eighth-period class? We need to sit and talk in the cafeteria about what we've seen. Ms. Neff, let's go out to eat!"

How could they be so energetic? I just wanted to slump in my office and prop up my tired feet. But my day's work of phone messages from parents, paper work, behavior reports, and the ordinary stuff of my job would be waiting.

The girls of today, as they piled out of the bus, were forced to make only one decision before them: would they go to their last class as Ms. Neff admonished, or cut class and pay the consequences?

My bus-birthed questions would remain far longer and press me to answer.

Must being female dictate restrictions on choices? Can my generation, which has not always chosen well, teach the next generation to choose well?

Can my generation, which has often believed that who we chose to marry defined our worth and very identity, teach the girls of today that God loves them precisely, exactly for who they are?

I confess that there are moments when I feel I have more questions than answers for the generation of young women following me. But I am optimistic about the big picture.

OUR CHALLENGE TO THINK

Myriads of options facing our young women are forcing us to think. While simplistic answers may serve when options are few, we who are older are having to think harder and get prepared to give better answers.

Two decades ago, as older women mentoring younger women, we might have given a pat answer to questions about abortion. Not so today. Our young women have heard the pro-choice messages, not only loudly and clearly, but often with reasonable-sounding arguments. Our youth have great skill at asking us tough questions, questions such as, "Why have incest, rape, and spouse abuse *not* become a rallying cry for churches to address in our society?"

I personally welcome questions. Our young women need our open dialogue and sometimes apologies for our actions or inaction. I find spiritual refreshment in having to dig deeper for reasons for my answers. Having to answer "I don't know" stimulates me out of my sometimes state of stagnation. The next generation tripping on our heels pushes us to climb higher.

As I paged through the completed surveys of the many women who responded, one comment appeared often: "Thank you for giving me this survey. It made me think." "Thanks for the challenge to think." You and I are not backing off from the struggle to think, explore, and grow.

I would like to encourage every woman who reads this book to become involved at some level, no matter how small, with a younger woman or girl. While the most obvious connection may be mothers and daughters, any woman can add a rich dimension to another younger person. As I counsel in my school I can guarantee that even if a teenage girl has a wonderful relationship with her mother, she will be richer still for connecting with another mentor.

Even the most healthy families experience glitches. Even with the best-matched moms and daughters, there are seasons when another woman's insights are invaluable.

ACCEPTING THE CHALLENGE

How do I begin? While no other person can tell you what younger woman to mentor, the following might help:

1. Pray for God to prepare you for the mentoring experience.
2. Ask Him to oversee the matching process.
3. Be alert to younger women around you and their apparent needs.
4. As you see opportunity, offer to help meet a need.
5. Be available to developing a relationship.

In my own experience, mentoring relationships have developed from:

- A phone call from a friend who needed another woman's

support for her daughter in crisis. (This young woman was willing to meet with me and a friendship developed that involved mentoring.)

- Opportunities to share holidays with relatives, resulting in correspondence and sharing times with younger women in the family.
- Previous students whom I met through my work.
- Networking in the body of believers.
- My mom/daughter relationship.

What do I do? Let the young friend in on my life. Yes, we talk. But mentoring is more. I share life stories. Let her know how I struggled through choices. Try these suggestions:

1. Take her to work with you, or to a place where you volunteer. Whether your friend or daughter is seven or seventeen, you can plan a day where she is your shadow in one place where God is using your gifts to impact your world. Christian women can call it a Deuteronomy Day (see Deuteronomy 6:7).

2. Adopt a friend or daughter for a non-workday. Welcoming another person into your routine helps her see a world bigger than her family's. I am grateful to women with different professions from mine who have talked to my daughter. They have broadened her perspectives and helped her see different ways God could use her gifts.

3. Take a young girl or young woman just for a "walk and talk," with emphasis on a shared activity. Plan a special excursion. It may be out for ice cream, a walk, to a museum, or for a bike ride. While future career and work may not be the focus of all conversation, it may season it. Girls are gleaning even when we are unaware; they listen, observe, visualize themselves in a different way with new information.

4. Include work and career in the Sunday school curriculum of your church for both girls and boys, honoring God's equality in creation.

5. Include seminars and workshops for women and girls related to their work. When girls see that Christian organizations take seriously the gifts and work of their women, they will learn that God values the work women do and their contribution to the world outside their home.

6. Stock your home and church library with materials that help girls and women discover their talents and gifts, as well as evaluate their preferences for careers.

7. Be real and open in talking about your struggles or those of your sisters and friends as they have made transitions in employment, perhaps struggled with self-support and survival, and made choices about training and careers.

8. Share facts as real facts. "Cinderella stories" do happen. But life for most of our daughters will be ordinary. God gives us an abundance of gifts, but I do not find magical glass slippers among them.

As we mentor younger women, when we feel overwhelmed by the challenges they face and the intensity of their struggles, we can share one common intergenerational bond: we still sing on school buses.

Remember the old hope chests? A young girl would begin collecting for her adult years: her first crocheted doily, a kitchen towel with painted initials. Mother, aunts, and grandmothers would add to the collection. A lidded box, mostly empty and kept in a closet, would become heavier every birthday. A recipe box, family favorites printed in each woman's distinctive scrawl or script. Fortunate girls might have a real hope chest, carved wood, cedar-lined. A well-stocked hope chest usually meant a young woman was ready for adulthood—meaning marriage and caring for a family.

My hope chest was a shoe box. Inside was my great-aunt Minnie's muffin recipe in her own handwriting. While the shoe box is long gone and the recipe card too, I remember sitting with

Aunt Minnie on her front porch eating those muffins. She talked as we swung gently.

"A lump of butter the size of an egg. You can let it set if you have to go do other things."

Then she might describe going to the field with her husband to help with animals or needing to do the milking. She was mentoring her great-niece on her priorities in life. You might say she was living a 1950s "Deuteronomy Day."

> Love the LORD your God with all your heart and with all your soul and with all your strength. These commandments that I give you today are to be upon your hearts. Impress them on your children. Talk about them when you sit at home and when you walk along the road, when you lie down and when you get up.
>
> Deuteronomy 6:5–7

Imagine that as you mentor you are adding to your young friend's hope chest—a 1990s hope chest for Christian living.

THE CHALLENGE FOR MOTHERS AND DAUGHTERS

Debra speaks:

As I worked with Miriam for nearly a year and a half on this book, I found myself watching my two daughters and wondering what, if anything, will these findings mean to them. As a Christian mother of two girls, how can I encourage them to think beyond cultural stereotypes? While raising them within a loving community of faith, how can I challenge them to question the traditional Christian assumptions regarding women's roles?

Without a doubt, things have changed for women in the last thirty years. My peers are the daughters of the women's movement. We witnessed the bra-burnings and strident rhetoric of militant feminists. We've seen the dualism of working women versus stay-at-home moms. We've watched the fall-out from the "have-it-all" myth: we *know* we can't "have it all"—we have to make choices or end up feeling like the cartoon character Wiley Coyote, spattered across the face of a cliff. Things have changed, but for the Christian woman, change continues to be met with resistance, traditional roles have been sanctified, and women continue to feel their church is slow to acknowledge their voice.

However, lest we fall victim to the easy assumption that secular society is ahead of the game while Christian circles lag behind, consider *these* statistics:[1]

- In school, boys are called on eight times more often than girls and in general receive more attention.[2]
- In 1992, 18,000 boys were eligible for National Merit Scholarships versus 8,000 girls.[3]
- In 1992, boys had higher scores than girls on eleven of fourteen subjects on the Scholastic Aptitude Test.[4]
- Worldwide, 76 million fewer girls than boys receive schooling.[5]
- Female education, rather than wealth of a country, influences its birthrate.[6]

As a mother of two daughters, these statistics are alarming. When I look at what the traditional church tells my girls, combined with cultural realities, I come face-to-face with the inevitable conclusion that unless I am *intentional* about the manner in which I parent, they will grow up experiencing the very reality I'm hoping to change. In her timely, delightfully pragmatic book *Raising Strong Daughters*, Jeanette Gadeberg writes,

> I have watched countless adult women come into counseling struggling with basic issues of low self-esteem, wavering self-identity, fears, and anxieties. . . . Today's women are expected to listen and adhere to the polarizing and conflicting messages they hear. Women are expected to define

their lives in opposing opposites depending on which group is doing the talking. . . . They are pressured to work outside the home in a full-blown career yet also to stay home and mother their children full-time. Some expect them to identify themselves as feminists, others snub this term as "too radical." Women can't win. . . . They are still managed by many rather than trained from an early age to listen to their own inner voice.[7]

I want to equip my daughters to "listen to their own inner voice," a voice that dates back to the prophet Isaiah when he wrote, "I have called you by name; you are mine" (43:1). Nonetheless, despite my early parenting resolve that I was going to raise my two daughters free of certain stereotypical gender biases, I find that their room is nonetheless cluttered with Barbie dolls, baby dolls, and more pink than I've seen outside of Baskin Robbins ice cream stores—and I have been the one most often making the purchases.

A LOVE AFFAIR WITH BARBIE

My daughters love Barbies, American Girl dolls, dress-up clothes, and virtually every other stereotypical toy marketed to little girls, just like millions of other prepubescent girls in America.

The love affair has lasted nine years. I haven't encouraged it. I haven't been at all overjoyed. In fact, my disdain is quite open and apparent. But the love affair continues.

Until my daughters' motor skills grew to match the intricate fittings of a Barbie's contemporary fashions, the ongoing frustration of "taking off and putting on" was the source of my intense dislike for this object of my children's affection—or so I thought. When they were finally able to clothe their assortment of Barbies and Kens with the assertion, "Mommy, I can do it myself!" I realized my dislike of the twelve-inch molded plastic with joints came from another source—and that source was within me.

Barbie represents every insecurity I've struggled with through the phases and stages of learning to live within my own skin. In short, she's everything I'm not. Perfect hair. Perfect face. Perfect body. Perfect life. Her choices have no consequences. She can change her career and identity as easily as changing outfits. I have made choices, and my life is defined by those choices. Although I would make many of the same choices again if given the chance, choosing one thing usually means choosing *not* to do something else. I'll never sing like Amy Grant or Kathy Trocolli (at least not in this lifetime!). I'll never be a vice president of marketing for a Fortune 500 company. I'm a mom, a writer, a wife (in no particular order of priority); I fight a perennial battle with an unwelcome ten pounds. I unwittingly hurt those I love and often fail to be the person I long to be. Unlike Barbie, my life is far from perfect.

Yet my daughters' love affair with this bastion of Americana is not nearly so complicated as my disdain. They are not thinking about what they are *not* in comparison to what Barbie is. When my daughters play with Barbies, they *are* whoever they are pretending Barbie to be. And their lives are limited only by where their imaginations can take them.

I made peace with my daughters' love affair while Christmas shopping in the toy department at Target. I stood staring at the wall of hot pink—Barbies in every imaginable configuration from Bedtime Barbies to Splashtime Skippers. The tug-of-war within me was going strong as I debated what would be under the Christmas tree: The outrageously expensive Bridal Barbie that was my daughter's heart's desire? Or the art easel *I* wanted her to have—a toy (I reasoned) that would encourage creativity and grow with her? I imagined my daughter's face on Christmas morning. Do I give her what *she* wants, or do I give her what *I* want her to have?

The Bridal Barbie went into the Target basket and under the tree. I realized that just as I don't want them to grow up with gender limitations, neither do I want to dictate who they are to become. God has His imprint on each one of my daughters. Who they are and who they were created to become has been woven beautifully into their personalities: their gifts, aptitudes, interests, and dreams. Within their imaginations are the sparks that will light their futures. My hope and desire is that I can encourage them to dream, to imagine, to widen the boundaries of what they consider possible. And in that effort, Barbie has become my ally, along with all their other dolls, dress-up clothes, games, and activities.

So along with the hot pink that colors their world, I am intentional about the gender roles they see modeled through very specific, though simple ways, such as,

- since infancy both the pediatrician and the dentist the girls see are women;
- I take them with me to my publisher's office, to Kinko's (my office away from home), and when I have brief meetings;
- my husband and I involve them in projects we're working on, letting them choose stories about themselves that we use in writing and speaking;
- my husband has taken them with him on pastoral calls to area hospitals.

As any mother knows, parenting is a humbling blend of who we are at our best—and worst. I approach each day with gratitude for the opportunity to "mother" these two little people, and a prayer for the grace to do so. And I echo Jeanette Gadeberg's belief that "we really can do something to help raise our daughters to become strong, confident, happy, independent women."

NOTES

1. The statistics quoted are from Jeanette Gadeberg, *Raising Strong Daughters* (Minneapolis: Fairview Press, 1995), p. 2. Original sources are cited following each statistic.
2. Myra Sadner and David Sadner, *Failing at Fairness: How America's Schools Cheat Girls* (New York: Scribner, 1994).
3. Quoted from Elizabeth Kennan, President of Mount Holyoke College, as cited in the Minneapolis-St. Paul *Star Tribune*, 14 February 1994.
4. Sadner and Sadner, op. cit.
5. *Population Action International Study*, a Washington, D.C., based nonprofit group as cited in the Minneapolis-St. Paul *Star Tribune*, 1 February 1994. "The more educated women are, the more likely they are to marry later, use birth control and have fewer, healthier children."
6. Ibid.
7. Gadeberg, op. cit., p. 3.

Part Three

Women Living a Covenant

"But whatever was to my profit I now consider loss for the sake of Christ. What is more, I consider everything a loss compared to the surpassing greatness of knowing Christ Jesus my Lord, for whose sake I have lost all things. I consider them rubbish, that I may gain Christ and be found in him, not having a righteousness of my own that comes from the law, but that which is through faith in Christ..."

Philippians 3:7–9

August 6, 1991. At the International Lutheran Conference on the Holy Spirit, Linda Rios Brook stood before five thousand people and declared, "How could I say I believed in God, and then give up teaching about Him just so I could keep a job? There was no choice for me: I had to resign.

"As I stand at this crossroads in my life, I am betting my life that God has His hand on this situation, and that God has His hand on me. And if that devotion to Jesus makes me appear foolish to the secular work, where my livelihood is, then a fool I am willing to be."

Linda Rios Brook

Seven

Living a Covenant

July 11, 1991. Linda Rios Brook, President and General Manager of KARE-11, the Minneapolis–St. Paul NBC affiliate, was summoned to Gannett Broadcasting's corporate offices in Washington, D.C. The summons came with short notice and cryptic comments. An article appearing in the *City Pages* was the topic of discussion. Puzzled but punctual, Linda arrived at the Twin Gannett Towers. As she rode the elevator up to Gannett's offices on the twenty-ninth floor, she wondered why a smear story about her in a regional giveaway tabloid would concern the executive management team of a national communications corporation with the stature of Gannett, publishers of *USA Today*.

Lunch waited in the expensively appointed offices overlooking the Potomac. She had no professional qualms about the meeting. Joining her soon would be Gannett's President of Broadcasting, Cecil Walker, and Ron Townsend, President of Television. She was a company "man," and they knew it. Madelyn Jennings, Vice President of Human Resources, was her professional mentor. Linda would be among friends.

A natural leader, articulate, intelligent, energetic, and blunt, Linda was committed to her work. She could make tough choices and manage well. She knew how to bring a station from the bottom of the ratings to the top rung. She was a turnaround gal.

She had spent fifteen years working up through the ranks of KENS-TV, San Antonio, Texas, to become president of that station. Under her leadership, the station was voted one of the top twenty-five best-managed television stations in the country. The owners of the Texas station transferred her to Jacksonville, Florida, to be a turnaround manager. She led WTLV-TV from number four to number two, sign-on to sign-off, and number one in certain key time periods, in only two years. Her influence was responsible for Gannett acquiring WTLV-TV. When Gannett acquired the Florida station, they knew they had an incredible asset in Linda Rios Brook. They wanted her in Minneapolis, Minnesota.

No problem. Linda had never been north of the Mason-Dixon line. She had no desire to be cold. But Linda was a "company man." If they wanted her in Minneapolis, that's where she would go. Linda moved to the cold country. When the job required relocating, Linda, her husband, and her two children moved. A family and a household moved—not just one person. Nobody doubted that Linda was a "company man." Her work was Number One in her life.

That's why Linda's three lunch partners enjoyed their meal. There would be none of the discomforts of conflict. No raised voices or arm twisting. Linda's answers were predictable.

The sun glistened on the Potomac. Gulls rose and dropped in the lazy heat of a July afternoon in the capital. Budgets, planning cycles, ratings. She had downsized the accounting department at KARE. They approved. Business conversation was interspersed with lighthearted banter.

Cecil and Ron joked about the media attention Linda generated no matter where she went, as someone recalled an observer at a golf tournament in Minneapolis who was struck by lightning.

"If you'd been there, you'd have been the one that was struck!"

Their laughter was comfortable.

"When you're the only female general manager of a large broadcasting group, you don't have to do anything to get attention except show up!" Linda responded.

They laughed, but she knew and they knew that they were not referring to gender. Being well-dressed and attractive, though she was both, was *not* her claim to attention and power. KARE–11 had moved from second place to first in the ratings and first in profitability. She was successful. She was effective. She was a turnaround gal.

Gannett sent Linda to Minnesota to make KARE profitable again. In the glory days of the 1980s, KARE was billing $50 million in advertising and enjoyed bloated operating expenses. Employees got healthy contracts and 10-percent raises. Parties and perks were the norm.

The economy changed. KARE failed to respond appropriately to economic realities. When Linda arrived, KARE's profits were nonexistent and ratings were unimpressive. She had her work cut out for her. Other television stations laid off entire bureaus. Linda did not downsize personnel; she reduced operation budgets, cut expenses, and lowered raises to 3 percent. But most jobs were saved. While some employees felt like growling stomachs on a diet, Linda did exactly what Gannett expected.

With one exception.

Brook always attracted attention. She was female in a male-dominated field; she was a change agent in status quo organizations. Her world view was decidedly Christian in a profession dominated by agnostics and humanists. Attention came to Linda like steel to a magnet, like lightning to the lightning rod on a high rise.

Gannett knew this. Part of her track record in Florida included being personally attacked by WAPE, a shock format or "blue" radio station. Her TV station advertised on "The APE" until it changed to the offensive shock format. Linda's station, WTLV-TV, had determined to be a community station. Its motto was "making good things happen for the first coast."

Linda made a simple, clear decision. No more advertising on The APE. Shock radio was not the format for community television advertising. Period.

Boom. The morning talk-show hosts on The APE took aim. Linda became one of their favorite targets. But her charisma and success prevailed. She emerged a wise survivor, not a victim.

The editor of *City Pages*, a Minneapolis tabloid, noticed her and decided that a woman with the scent of a Christian running a major media organization was worth exploring. A reporter was assigned.

City Pages is a free-distribution alternative newspaper; mainstream it is not. The assigned reporter began showing up at the places Linda frequented in her "off-work" hours, which frequently involved podiums with microphones and large audiences.

Public speaking is not unusual for broadcasting personalities and community leaders. Serving on philanthropic boards, public speaking for community organizations, and active participation in community events, country clubs, political and social fundraising, and pursuing other personal interests are not only common, but encouraged for individuals in leadership positions.

But tabloid reporters don't shadow them, because those activities are politically correct. Linda was not. Her podium and microphone were used for politically incorrect purposes: she was a Bible teacher.

Tabloids are not well known for factual reporting or even-handed presentation. The reporter carefully chose phrases that distorted the facts. Incomplete reporting squeezed out truth.

City Pages reported that Brook had made KARE-11's newsroom a "place of turmoil" with "a severe crisis in morale."

Fact: The "dispirited" reporters in this tumultuous newsroom produced a 10:00 P.M. newscast that topped the ratings.

City Pages said that Brook would practice hiring discrimination. Corporate leadership should not be subjected to the risk of having a Christian at the top.

Fact: *City Pages* failed to turn up any example of hiring discrimination. (What if Linda had been Jewish? or black? or Native American? or lesbian?)

City Pages implied that Linda's religious conduct might influence the news.

Fact: A vice-president who worked closely with Linda for two years at KARE stated that she never forced her views on anyone—including the news department. Newsroom employees agreed that Brook had never tried to influence newsroom policies or practices with her religious views.

City Pages accused her of being anti-Semitic.

Fact: The vice-president called this absolutely bunk, as did her other co-workers I interviewed. The complete texts of Linda's speeches fail to support this accusation.

The reporter did what tabloid reporters do: created misimpressions and half-truths from phrases lifted out of context from speeches, statements, and public appearances. And, in fact, when interviewed later a spokesperson for *City Pages* admitted they were unable to support a single, valid smoking gun. But never mind that technicality; that's tabloid freedom of speech.

None of this is surprising to people who expect tabloids to be tabloids. Major newspapers and weekly news magazines seldom look to tabloids for noteworthy stories, particularly *regional* tabloids. They don't typically reprint information that Elvis was sighted or copy pictures of multi-limbed people.

But the story about Linda caused media heads to turn. Major newspapers and Gannett took notice of the *City Pages* story and a media frenzy followed. A *St. Paul Pioneer Press* column about Brook was entitled, "KARE's Brook out on a wing and a prayer?"

She wasn't simply a public person acting as spokesperson for United Way or the March of Dimes. She wasn't simply a keynote speaker for a metropolitan Rotary club. She was a spokesperson for the Christian faith. She led Bible studies; she talked openly and publicly about her faith; she was an outspoken Christian woman in the business end of broadcast media. Her intuition told her a values conflict was brewing—and that's why she was summoned to the Twin Gannett Towers in Washington, D.C.

The meeting continued. They acknowledged that she was doing a great job. Profitability was up, expenses were down, ratings were rising. As president and general manager of the NBC affiliate, she earned over $250,000 annually. She was a valued person in a company whose motto was "a world of difference where many voices speak."

Gannett chose to listen to a tabloid.

After lunch the focus of the friendly foursome changed. The questions were not, "How can we change the focus of the attention you're getting?" or, "What evidence can you offer us and the press that these allegations are untrue?"

They wanted to know how much time Linda spent on this "stuff." What *was* her faith? What did she believe? What was the difference between fundamentalism and evangelicalism? Where did she get her information? Occasionally, they left her alone to confer privately.

Linda walked to the window and took in the panoramic view. Arlington Cemetery. The white columns of the Robert E. Lee home. The spire of the Washington Monument. The flying buttresses of the National Cathedral. She looked out over the capital of a society founded on religious tolerance.

The threesome reentered.

"Linda, don't you think that it's more normal to *attend* church rather than to '*do*' church?" she was asked.

After all, this was Linda Rios Brook, an administrator who could and would negotiate anything, who had given 150 percent for her job time and again, who had given up temperate climates and Florida beaches to survive wind chills of thirty degrees below zero. They could not comprehend that Linda believed in anything but the Company Way.

"Linda, this is the sort of thing that loonies do," she was told.

Late in the afternoon, John Curly, Chief Executive Officer of the Gannett Group, joined the meeting.

"What are you doing with all this religion business?" John asked her within two minutes.

"I teach a Bible class. I speak to Christian churches on matters of faith. My specialties are apologetics and historical interpretation. I do not address social or political issues."

"Don't do it again."

"Don't do what?" Linda's question was unexpected.

"Don't teach or preach." John's matter-of-fact, non-negotiable manner did not change.

Neither did Linda's.

She continued with an explanation that Ron, Madelyn, Cecil, and John had not expected to hear.

"While some managers spend their free time playing golf or whatever, I spend mine teaching Bible classes. I have always done this. It is not new, nor is it news to the company," Linda said.

"I knew it, but I never liked it," came John's response.

Dusk cast shadows on the Gannett Twin Towers. The gulls floating over the Potomac no longer glistened white but appeared a dull gray.

Linda continued. Though her audience was a tiny foursome, their response would be read by thousands.

"In a company whose motto is 'a world of difference where many voices speak,' I would hope there would be room for diversity."

"There is not. Don't do it again," John said and rose abruptly to leave.

The meeting was over. He had accomplished what he intended to do in this meeting. The CEO of the Gannett Group, an international firm that employed 36,000 people, fully believed he had silenced Brook's voice.

Though Linda wanted desperately to believe she had not heard him correctly, her realism prevailed. She stood and with practiced professionalism, thanked him for his time.

"By the way," John continued, "congratulations on your May results; you're doing a nice job."

His compliment was small comfort.

As Cecil and Ron drove Linda to the airport, they put the finishing touches on John's directive. She was to put this matter behind her quickly and quietly, canceling any further speaking engagements, including teaching at her church. They wanted this annoying controversy cleared away quickly, like dirty dishes after dinner.

She got out of the car, said her good-byes, and walked into the airport. Her usual preflight nausea went unnoticed; the airport white noise was unheard. She was in shock. She realized her options were grim.

WHEN OUR LIVES SPIN OUT OF CONTROL

Although the drama played out in a posh office overlooking the Potomac may have involved higher stakes than most of us have to face, in many ways Linda's story is every woman's story: unpredictable turns of events, choices in which neither option looks good, financial pressures, conflicts between personal values and corporate cultures.

As Christian women we are not immune to the unexpected,

the devastating, the difficulties of living, loving, working, and serving. The events that spin our lives out of control are as diverse as our life situations.

We walk into a meeting with our supervisor and are stunned by unanticipated developments. We're given notice that our company has been bought by another corporation; personnel changes, restructuring, and layoffs are imminent. Our boss drives us crazy with attention to unnecessary details or is simply incompetent. We face situations involving questionable ethics, or we're asked to participate in programs or policies that conflict with our values.

Or what about events in our personal lives that throw us a curve? Our marriages strain, tensions rise, and talk of divorce or separation emerges. A loved one is diagnosed with a serious illness—or we discover a small lump while taking a shower. We get a call in the middle of the night with news that our teenager is somewhere doing something we never dreamed we would have to confront.

Does being a Christian make any difference when things don't go our way? When our world seems to fall apart? When the unthinkable happens? When our worst fear materializes into stark reality?

Being a Christian gives us no reprieve from facing humanity's challenges, heartaches, and changes in our work, our families, and our faith. Christian women are fired, stressed out, overworked, and underpaid. We make costly mistakes, argue with our spouses, lose our temper with our kids, get to work late. We have no guarantees. We're human—and so is everyone around us. So what difference does this thing called faith make? Or more to the point, does our commitment to Christ make any difference—at work, in our families, in our innermost thoughts—in times of crisis and difficult decisions? Did a commitment to Christ make a difference for Linda Rios Brook?

WHEN COMMITMENT COUNTS

Resigning didn't make economic sense. Her husband's job had been eliminated due to downsizing, her son was in a private college, and her daughter was in high school. Unemployment was not an attractive option. She could stop teaching and keep her job. She would still be a Christian. She could attend church, tithe, go to inspirational functions, and keep a low profile.

But that wouldn't be true to who she was, a grim prospect for a person like Linda.

She could continue teaching and fight to keep her job. She could sue and go to court with a strong prospect of winning.

"But what would I gain?" she asked herself. "If I won and they were forced to take me back, where would I be? The company did not stand by me. They chose not to. If I took legal action and won, why would I *want* to work for them?"

Linda had two options and neither was good: be silent and keep her job; continue speaking and lose her job.

"Linda Rios Brook, a visible evangelical Christian who became president and general manager of KARE-TV (Gannett-owned Channel 11) in May 1989, has been replaced by Hank Price, president and general manager of Gannett's station in Greensboro, North Carolina."[1]

A statement by Ron Townsend, President of Gannett, said that Brook had resigned "to pursue a different career challenge and other goals."[2]

"According to sources close to the situation, Gannett has apparently told Brook to decide whether she wants to be a minister or the leader of a commercial television station."[3]

"A religious discrimination lawsuit is rumored to be pending. If Brook files a religious discrimination suit, it's very possible that she would win, according to John Whitehead, President of the Rutherford Institute, a civil liberties organization specializing in the defense of religious liberty."[4]

While the press coverage continued, Linda sought counsel and prayed.

But more important than her aversion to working for a company that didn't support her, she *knew* what the media does with stories about Christians. She had watched from the inside. They print stories about Christians only when they've done something illegal, illogical, or outlandish.

The media have portrayed Christians as hysterical, uneducated fundamentalists disrupting school board meetings and burning books. They've portrayed priests as perverts and nuns as narrow-minded nitwits. They've highlighted the most vocal of quiet demonstrators and televangelists who fleece their own flock. Linda did not wish to supply grist for fanatical Christian stereotypes.

What intelligent, articulate, natural leader would want to offer herself to such a pool of piranhas?

She chose to resign without suing.

She chose to join the ranks of the unemployed with the freedom to speak. She knew this meant humiliation, grief, and depression, and she experienced each emotion in waves.

While she consciously chose to resign, she says that in another sense she had no choice. "How could I say I believed in God, and then give up teaching about Him just so I could keep a job? There was no choice for me: I had to resign."

August 6, 1991. At the International Lutheran Conference on the Holy Spirit, Linda stood before five thousand people and declared, "As I stand at this crossroads in my life, I am betting my life that God has His hand on this situation, and that God has His hand on me. And if that devotion to Jesus makes me appear foolish to the secular work, where my livelihood is, then a fool I am willing to be."

Obviously, Linda's significant choice was not when she arrived at the crossroads. It was the moment she chose to believe that Jesus Christ was not just a good person in history, a better idea for improved relationships, a crutch when you've taken a nasty stumble. She had chosen to believe that Jesus was both human and divine—God and man—exactly who He said He was.

On August 11, six corporate officers flew to the Twin Cities in their private jet. Cecil Walker, Ron Townsend, and a few others arrived in the morning and ensconced themselves in Linda's office. They instructed Dick Modig, a manager with seniority, to call all staff to the stage for a noon meeting.

Cecil read a very brief announcement that Linda had resigned to "pursue other career interests." No explanation. The staff was told that no conversation about the matter was expected.

The new president, Hank Price, was introduced, and the staff was invited to ask Hank any questions they might have. Silence. Everyone went back to work. The "Linda mess" had been erased. Their media problem was gone.

"It was eerie," said Pame Gardner, one of Linda's co-workers. Pame went on to describe what happened during the meeting. "While we were in that meeting, every item that identified Linda was removed. The plaque from her door, her parking space identification, even company pictures that included her. It was as if when we went back to work, she didn't exist anymore."

Within months, "Linda supporters" were removed, including Pame.

The person about whom Cecil Walker had once said, "She can have any job in broadcasting she wants if she plays her cards right" had been banished. The only remaining evidence that she had worked there was a sleek, profitable budget and the Twin Cities' number-one-rated 10 P.M. newscast, a rating which was the direct result of Linda's influence and the changes she implemented.

THE ROAD NOT TAKEN

While poets have eloquently described the difference our choices make and the mystery of what might have been, Robert Frost's words are particularly appropriate: "I took the [road] less traveled by, and that has made all the difference."[5]

As a result of Linda's absence from their ranks, KARE-TV has a new competitor. Within one week after Linda's resignation from the NBC affiliate, she was approached to become a part of a team with a different mission for television.

She did not instantly move into a new office with President and General Manager on the door. Fairy tales are written that way. Although the God Linda trusted is capable of miraculous timing, time is His tool, not His master. Linda's career transition took months.

A team with a different mission obtained ownership of KTMA Channel 23 on February 29, 1992. The investors acquired the bankrupt independent station for 3.3 million dollars, renamed it KLGT-TV and organized it as Sonlight Television, a reference to Jesus: "Minnesota's Family Station offering quality TV for the entire family."

"For years," says Linda, "I've listened as some colleagues have told parents that broadcasters aren't responsible for what kids watch on TV. Hogwash!

"TV does have a social responsibility. At Sonlight we want to turn television back into a friend of the family."[6]

As we hear Linda say those words with her customary directness, we recognize she could never have been so bold on the twenty-ninth floor of the Gannett Twin Towers. She had to keep her beliefs separate from her work. Had she spoken up, she would have been voted down, silenced. She is free now, not only to speak, but to plan, direct, and manage with a mission.

"Some say that we've gone too far and that television cannot be turned around," Linda says. "Perhaps they are right. But Sonlight wants to try.

"What is a Christian television station? It is a television station owned and operated by Christians. It is not twenty-four hours of 'preaching,' although there will be thoughtful, well-produced programs that proclaim the Christian message. It is not Christian radio with pictures. It is a television station that will present Christians as they really are: normal. Normal people doing normal things, normal situations, good times, bad times, funny times, tough times.

"The purpose of Sonlight is to provide family television for the Twin Cities; programming which entertains, informs, and educates within the context of traditional Christian values.

"The vision of Sonlight is to provide access and give voice to the Christian perspective on social issues, government, education, and economics. It's a tall order. It can't happen all at once. I find the possibility that it can happen at all a more sobering thought. But it cannot happen unless the Christian community supports the effort."[7]

Forever the woman sought by the media, Linda was contacted by a reporter her first Monday morning at KLGT-TV. Sonlight Television had just closed the legal transaction on Saturday, gaining ownership, and a *Star Tribune* reporter was full of questions.

She assured him that they were not going to shock anyone. The ownership and management team at KLGT-TV intended to provide family entertainment.

"What television is supposed to do a good part of the time is just be a friend. It's supposed to be entertainment without shocking your sensitivities into the Twilight Zone or something you're afraid is destroying the society you live in."

"What KTMA programs might get the boot?" asked Noel Holston, staff writer for the Minneapolis *Star Tribune.*

"Some paid programming probably will be inappropriate for us to continue," Linda answered. "If we have any of the '1–900-GIRL' lines and those sorts of things, that goes immediately. I don't know if there is any of that. To tell the truth, we closed on Saturday, we're here on Monday morning, and we're trying to figure out what we've got."

Programming that was brought into KLGT-TV's line-up included *Barney Miller, Sanford and Son, Good Times, 227, Different Strokes, The Hogan Family,* and *The Man From U.N.C.L.E.* They also added *Saved by the Bell,* an acclaimed multicultural series for teens.

Linda's challenges in her new job were big and bold. Previous contracts were still contracts requiring patience by the new station's audience while Linda directed her efforts at changing the format. Under Linda's leadership the station had to make a profit.

She communicated with the station's audience, letting them know, "This is a ministry, but it is also a business. We have a chance to make a difference. Please give us time to do it."

It took time. But by any new business standards, it was fast. KLGT-TV's ink changed from red to black in October 1992.

A Covenant of Faith

"As I stand at this crossroads in my life, I am betting my life that God has His hand on this situation, and that God has His hand on me."

When things were not going the way Linda would have hoped, planned, or anticipated, when she had more questions than answers, when an exceptional career seemed to have ended, Linda did not diminish the difficulty of what had happened. But her words clearly reflected something more important than planned results, answers to inevitable questions, or a successful career.

As I stand at this crossroads in my life, I am betting my life that God has His hand on this situation, and that God has His hand on me.

Linda was living a covenant of faith. Even when her world

was falling apart, she bet her world on the God of Abraham and Sarah; she bet her world on Jesus, His Son, the Risen Lord.

In this section we will be looking at women and our faith, our lives in the churches we attend, and our spirituality. But faith and spirituality are widely used words with multiple meanings. When we say that Linda Rios Brook was living a covenant of faith, what do we mean by that? What exactly is a "covenant of faith"?

Let's suppose, for a moment, you were to go on a contract search in your home, what would you find? You might find a loan agreement for your car, a rental agreement, or a mortgage coupon book for your home. Utilities, cable television, investments, charge cards. Most of us have signed a stack of contracts. We've probably forgotten a handful that were important to us at one time: tuition commitments, insurance, health care payments. Some of us have even signed prenuptial agreements.

Now let's go on a covenant search. Most of us would complete our search empty-handed. "Covenant" is an old-fashioned word. Not only is it an old-fashioned word, it is an old-fashioned idea. A covenant is a mutually binding agreement. A covenant stands whether both sides keep their part of the agreement or not.

A contract stands only as long as both parties meet the terms of the agreement. If one breaks her or his part, the other is free. The contract is no longer binding.

No wonder contracts are more popular today than covenants. Contracts are not forever; there *is* a way out. Contracts are only as strong as the commitments of each party, which means they are as weak as the commitment of the *least* committed party.

In contrast, covenants are forever. Covenants are an inside thing. Keeping a covenant depends on what's in us, not what's happening around us.

In Isaiah, we are told,

"Fear not, for I have redeemed you;
    I have called you by name; you are mine.
When you pass through the waters,
    I will be with you;
and when you pass through the rivers,
    they will not sweep over you.
When you walk through the fire,
    you will not be burned;
    the flames will not set you ablaze.
For I am the LORD, your God,
    the Holy One of Israel, your Savior . . ."

Isaiah 43:1–3

When Linda said, "I am betting my life that God has His hand on this situation, and that God has His hand on me," her confidence was born of knowing that God's promise, God's covenant with people of faith, is stronger than any circumstances. *I have called you by name; you are mine.* God knows the particulars. God knows how we feel when the odds are against us. God knows our fears when we feel overwhelmed. He knows our reluctance when we fear being burned. As Christian women, we are people of the covenant, a covenant as personal as our name, as non-negotiable as the saving grace of Jesus Christ's resurrection.

When we write about faith, spirituality, or covenant, we are defining these terms within the biblical tradition.

"It stands to reason, doesn't it, that if the alive-and-present God who raised Jesus from the dead moves into your life, he'll do the same thing in you that he did in Jesus, bringing you alive to himself?" (Roman 8:9a, 10, The Message).

What does an "alive-and-present God" have to do with workplace issues, decision making, and putting our lives back together when we face difficulties? How does this faith thing make a difference for women in the workplace and in our relationships? Simply this: we can be confident that God is in control. We can trust Him in any and every decision. Our covenant of faith means we don't have to know the outcome; when we act, choose, or decide in faith, we can leave the results to God. But let's get back to specifics. Let's translate being connected to our alive-and-present God to our real-life experiences. Let's talk a little further with Linda Rios Brook.

NOTES

1. *Twin Cities Christian*, (22 August 1991).
2. Ibid.
3. *St. Paul Pioneer Press* (9 August 1991).
4. *Twin Cities Christian* (22 August 1991).
5. Robert Frost, *The Road Not Taken* (New York: Henry Holt and Company, 1951), p. 271.
6. *Twin Cities Christian*, (19 March 1992).
7. Ibid.

Eight

Never Forever the Same

A fter experiencing something that turns your life upside down, how are you different?

I love asking that question of women who have experienced dramatic changes in their lives. At first I expected profound, philosophical responses. Instead, without exception, I hear simple, mundane—and incredibly interesting answers. (The profound often comes much later after several more questions and cups of coffee.)

Linda Rios Brook was faced with a situation in which there were no good alternatives. No matter what she decided, the negatives outweighed the positives—or so it seemed. But God had a plan. And Linda was willing to trust, to risk, to move on.

When I asked Linda, "How are you different?" her response was both surprisingly simple and beautifully hopeful:

I'm not afraid of flying anymore. I know that sounds strange. But because of my family background, I have an overdeveloped sense of responsibility. I have always be-

lieved that I was responsible for the outcome of everything
in life. Therefore, I necessarily had a lot of silly fears. One
of them was flying.

I worried that because I flew a lot I might die in a crash,
and then who would raise my children? But of all the fears
I ever had, the greatest was that I would make poor choices
and destroy my career. Therefore, I worked harder and
worried more to be sure that my professional competence
was beyond reproach.

As Job said, "That which I greatly feared has happened
to me." As a result of having my greatest fear come to pass,
my other fears have mostly disappeared. I fear God, but not
much else. That has been a strange outcome of all of this.

As a child, Linda came home to no electricity because of un-
paid bills. She was accustomed to notices that the family had to
move because of neglected finances. Her stepfather and alcoholic mother were unable to give her that inner sense of security—that tomorrow will be okay. Children of alcoholics take on
the mantle of "I have to do it all. No one else can be trusted. I
will always put food on my own table. I *will* have financial security."

Linda's husband, Larry Brook, had a different philosophy.
While Linda wanted to "stock up for a cold winter's day," Larry
felt more financial freedom.

"Debt was a ton of lead to Linda," he says, "and it actually
was a point of contention early in our marriage."

One of few friction points, I might add. They married in
1980, both program directors of television stations. They shared
professional interests as well as ideas about family and God. At
one time, their parallel careers included sharing office staff and
conference rooms.

After Gannett gave Linda the ultimatum and told her "to
think on it" on "sick leave," she accompanied Larry on a business trip to California. They talked and talked. He says that

walking through it with Linda was a strengthening experience. Larry had seen the impact of Linda's childhood and the deep fears that simply were a given. He knew her fear of being unemployed, her fear of no security and no guarantees for the future.

While he worked, Linda drove up into the mountains around Sacramento. She spent some time one afternoon sitting on a rock overlooking a scenic lake, wondering what would happen next. She speculated about the media frenzy going on in Minneapolis. As her anxiety rose, she complained to God. He assured her that He had taken her out of the fray and brought her to this beautiful spot to experience peace, not anxiety.

A profound and unlikely thing was happening. This child of an alcoholic was learning to trust. Her world was in turmoil; Linda felt inner peace.

GETTING A GRIP: HISTORY'S HAND ON THE FUTURE

Closure, congruence. Psychologists and therapists tell us that healthy living includes putting the past in some sort of believable perspective, something that we can accept and with some degree of comfort, leave behind us. Otherwise, the "stuff" of our history becomes baggage. Mental health professionals tell us that in order to live each day with balance and face the future, we cannot hang on to past hurts.

Carrying the past with us is like trying to hurry through a crowded airport with a large bulky purse hanging on one shoulder, newspaper under the arm, and a cup of coffee in one hand while pulling an oversized piece of luggage with the other hand, luggage that insistently lists to one side with one wheel going in a different direction than the other three.

Excess baggage. It's simply hard to move ahead with it.

Linda certainly had a right to pull excess baggage: anger, injustice, discrimination, humiliation. Grief, economic uncertainty, depression, and the prospect of boredom were very real fears she faced daily.

Yet she has refused permanent residence to any of these emotions. Yes, they are real. Yes, these emotions try to revisit her. But she looks at her crossroads through a faith perspective, a perspective that provides some answers, while some very real questions remain unanswered.

She prays for the reporter of *City Pages* who wrote the infamous article. We might expect that of one who follows Jesus, because His teaching includes forgiveness. One child who had solemnly memorized the Lord's Prayer quietly prayed, "And forgive us our trash-passing as we forgive those who pass trash against us."

Forgiving the trash-passing has been part of Linda's healing.

She knew that if she chose to sue Gannett for violating her first amendment rights of free speech, she would have many supporters. Chuck Colson spoke out on his national radio show about the injustice she had suffered due to the dominant elite in our culture who persistently infringe on the rights of Christians these days. No one, he says, blows the whistle.

Dr. Morris Vaagenes, pastor of one of the largest churches in Minnesota, supported her through her toughest days. Though he supports Linda's decision not to sue and has no sense of vindictiveness toward KARE-TV, he would have supported her had she chosen to call them to justice.

Perhaps, had she become embroiled in a court battle, which would have been emotionally draining, dirty, and delightful for *City Pages*, she would not have been able to embrace her new mission with vigor.

She did not hesitate to get back into the foray of broadcasting. Though God does not always call women back into the same careers or relationships, He does *not* put them on a shelf marked "unusable." She says she does not need a full answer for why. She has adequate answers to do her work today.

Why? I don't know why. I don't accept that this happened to me so that others will be encouraged. That's lunacy. Who would be encouraged by the devastation of a person's career? "Become a Christian and you, too, can be publicly humiliated and unemployed." That won't get a lot of recruits.

No, there's another reason. Perhaps it has to do with Sonlight Television. Perhaps it has to do with my speaking and teaching ministry. Perhaps it's both. Perhaps it's neither. But it doesn't matter. I am certain of this. The God I serve is a sovereign God. I am a servant. Not a perfect servant, but I have tried to be obedient, and I have tried to be faithful within my understanding. Therefore, this God I serve can be trusted with my life. He doesn't play games. He doesn't wreak havoc in His children's lives to teach them a lesson. I reject that concept out of hand.

When something like this is allowed to occur, it is for a reason. In some way, God is going to glorify His own purpose and I will be restored. God tested me for a purpose. I hope I passed. If I did, when He reveals the reason, it will be clear, and we won't have to wonder whether that was the reason or not. In the meantime, He has been faithful to the things that mattered to me.

Events like Linda's crossroads often bring people together who become unexpected partners in unpredictable ways. Dr. Morris Vaagenes, who was neither broadcaster nor previous mentor, became a friend and fellow visionary. He was one of the pastors whose advice she sought after she had been given the ultimatum by Gannett to be silent about her religious beliefs.

Linda, her husband, Larry, Dan Morstad, and Dr. Vaagenes met and discussed the dilemma. He did not give her advice but offered her a verse from Scripture. He was pastor of the North Heights Lutheran Church and as such had been invited to the White House during the Reagan administration to be one of twenty-five pastors providing input on the prayer amendment. He was also co-chairman of the International Lutheran Conference on the Holy Spirit. He had asked Linda to be their plenary speaker on August 6, prior to her July interrogation in Washington, D.C. While extending this invitation was an ordinary function for him, it was NOT ordinary for him to invite women to any battlefield. This was Linda's first speaking commitment after being given the silence ultimatum. To show up and fulfill his invitation was to run a personal gauntlet.

She did. To Vaagenes's credit, he offered to withdraw the invitation in order to remove Linda from an apparently "no-win" situation. She declined his offer. Perhaps something in her corresponded to an ancient queen's intuition.

Queen Esther was told that perhaps she was in her position of conflict mixed with power for "such a time as this." Her response was, ". . . if I perish, I perish" (Esther 4:16). Linda knew her crossroads had arrived. Her speech included these words:

> I've come to a turning point in my life, for the options that are available to me are not particularly attractive. In order to be acceptable to some who believe that Christians in media are somehow suspect, I must either be silent about my Christian faith or risk being thought a fool, a zealot, and even a bigot, by people whose approval I greatly desire to have. So I've come here this morning to tell you that I know what it's like to be called to holy worldliness in an environment that grows increasingly more hostile to Christians, and to tell you that while I may be again badgered in the tabloid press for what I am about to say, I shall nonetheless say it! I am not ashamed of the Gospel of Jesus Christ!

She could only imply to the thousands of listeners that her coming to speak had far-reaching implications. Though few may remember her words, none will ever forget what was most significant. She walked up to the microphone and spoke.

The conclusion of her speech was not the end. Dr. Vaagenes told the crowd that she reminded him of Martin Luther. A sense of significance charged the room. In that emotional moment the standing ovation drowned out the voice that had said, "Don't do it again."

She ignored the voice of the CEO whom she respected. She listened to the voice of the One whom she loved.

LINDA'S LESSON FOR US

I asked Linda what she would like women to remember from her experience. Her response? "Thou shalt not kid thyself."

> I am very concerned that many people who say they are Christians don't know very much about their faith because they are scripturally illiterate. When their choices come, and they certainly will, many people will be caught in a trap because their beliefs are philosophical or emotional more than factually based. They don't know what real Christianity is supposed to look like. Going "through the fire and flood," or going "to the cross" are phrases.
>
> Every sane person worships something. And the god they worship will manifest at the time of crisis when life-altering decisions are to be made. At this point of decision, many will be surprised at how quickly they abandoned their professed faith in God to place their trust in something else: a relationship, a job.
>
> In our modern lives, there are indicators of our state of being that can tell us where we are. For example, there is a "body fat" test to tell us if we are at risk for stroke or heart disease. There are tests we can take to tell us if we are at risk for alcoholism, drug abuse, depression, etc. There is also a set of indicators to let us know where we are spiritually.
>
> I learned long ago that if a person wants to know what she really worships in life, she could find out by taking her checkbook and her calendar. Wherever she spent her dis-

cretionary time and her discretionary income and where she spent her thoughts, there would be the God she worshiped. I think a person does not know Jesus as Savior unless he also knows Him as Lord.

Thou shalt not kid thyself.

Another way to find out what is important to a person is to ask those closest to them. Kirsten Rios, Linda's sixteen-year-old daughter, describes her mom this way:

> You know how little girls say, "My mom is the prettiest person in the world"? Well, my mom is a real mom. She proved her words. She stood up and proved her point.
>
> She has done so many remarkable things. She is really worried about our world. She cares about other young kids. The people at KARE—she did a lot of sacrifices for those people. And the one who really CARED had to leave.

Kirsten speaks with pride, but also with a perspective that life isn't all glowing. She describes the whole event as a trauma that is much nicer to look back on, but definitely was not good while going through it. She says that it made her question her faith, but God "proved a lot and everything came together. God wasn't going to throw her career down the toilet," Kirsten observed with genetic bluntness. "He doesn't do hocus-pocus." (I sensed the baton of communication as well as of conviction was being passed on.)

She says it was an adjustment always having her mom around the house for the following eight months or so after being accustomed to her being at the office. Nonetheless, it is obvious that respect and friendship survived.

As I interviewed people about Linda, I kept hearing the same word: COURAGE. A man who worked with her who does not share her religious values called her "decisive, an excellent communicator, a clear manager, but most of all courageous."

COURAGE. The description was echoed by Dr. Paul

Ramseyer (a leading Christian broadcaster in the Midwest), Dr. Morris Vaagenes, co-workers like Pame Gardner, the Morstads, and literally hundreds who know of her experience.

What moment required the most courage? It might well have been that first speech she gave after being told to be silent. I imagine that to rise from your seat on the platform and walk to a microphone would be a long, long walk—when all you've worked for will be taken away when you open your mouth. I have heard the tape of that event, and indeed there is an ever-so-slight quiver in Linda's voice as she delivered her "gauntlet" speech. It was followed by a standing ovation by thousands and merited commendations by her supporters.

Another moment of courage was quite different. She was to go to the studio of KARE-TV and tell the assembled staff in the presence of Gannett's powerbrokers and the newly assigned president that she had "chosen to resign to pursue other interests." She refused to make that statement because it was not true.

Instead she stayed home, took the phone off the hook, and washed her dog. I believe that Linda Brook shampooing her dog wearing her jeans and baggy shirt rather than standing before her former staff in impeccable, professional attire, mouthing what her heart knew was a lie was as much an act of courage as walking to that microphone to give her gauntlet speech.

I am thankful for the steps of courageous women these days. I am thankful for their words. I'm encouraged to know of the brave, not-so-public acts of courage. The day Linda stayed home in silence is evidence of her integrity.

"To thine own self be true," wrote Shakespeare.

Linda remained true to herself, true to her Lord. She had once said to a reporter who queried her as an exceptional female leader, "Don't get into a position where you're protected, where there's not opportunity for you to fail." From traffic director, to news producer, to director of advertising for a theater group, from promotion director, to program director and station president, Linda was always in a position where she could fail.

Linda lived her own words.

She faced the risk of failure.

She became a target when she chose to be a leader.

She faced the risk of being misunderstood.

She became a survivor when others called her a victim.

Her options included retaliation. She chose to move on.

She faced a challenging crossroads and chose to be a woman of courage.

Christian women in the workplace are making a difference because we are covenant keepers. We are committed beyond contracts. We are keeping covenants with no visible guarantees. Our choices are different. Our priorities are different. Our actions are different.

Women who love God are on the move. Change has buffeted and strengthened us. Surprises of life, crisis, and challenge beyond our dreams have not silenced or stopped us. Christian women are making a difference. Our presence is being felt in new and different ways in the marketplace—and in our churches. The difference we are making in our churches and what 1,000 covenant keepers have to say about their church experience is where we will turn our attention next.

Nine

Where We Serve, Where We Pray

D *ebra speaks:*
"Nance . . ." His voice cracked on the other end of the phone. "Nance, Leigh died this afternoon."

The phone call was not unexpected, but the timing was awful. A week before Easter. A week before churches everywhere celebrated new life and resurrection, hope and anticipation. A week before Easter, Nancy's best friend had died.

Four years before her death, Leigh began having neurological problems. Her doctors initially ruled out major concerns, but tests were inconclusive. They were unable to determine what was causing the difficulties. Leigh was a young wife with a one-year-old baby. Her life was busy—too busy to be sick. The neurological problems came and went, probably nothing to worry about, so she changed diapers, rocked her little one to sleep, and went on with her life.

Nancy and Leigh had met in college. At nineteen and twenty, they were high on ideals, short on cash, and long on dreams of what their future would hold. They became inseparable friends until romance put miles between them. Leigh stayed in California. Nancy left the beaches, year-round suntans, and temperate weather for a young man named Mark, who was attending graduate school in Minnesota. But the miles between Minnesota and California didn't distance the friendship. Their early-married experiences and first pregnancies were shared via long distance phone calls and frequent letters.

Leigh's neurological problems persisted. Blurred vision. Headaches. Dizziness. Two years after the problems began, the doctors finally discovered what was causing the distress. A tumor was wrapped around her optic nerve. When Leigh's cancer was diagnosed, Nancy's parents paid for an airline ticket and she flew to California to be with her friend. They told stories, shared memories, laughed, and cried. They talked about the reality of an abbreviated future.

"So, Leigh, what's the prognosis?" Nancy asked with characteristic bluntness.

"Not good," she replied, her voice emotionless. "The tumor is inoperable. Treatment might help, might give me a few more months, but the doctors say we're talking months, not years."

Nancy heard her friend's words, listened to the matter-of-fact voice, and wanted to scream, "Leigh, don't be so clinical! You're telling me you're going to die, and you're too young to die! You have a baby, a husband—and you're my best friend. I don't want you to die!"

Two years went by in a blur of doctors' appointments, ineffective treatments, and the inevitable never out of mind. The disease progressed quickly. Leigh was dead at thirty-three.

The phone call was surprisingly brief. A few succinct words: "Leigh died this afternoon." Nancy hung up the telephone and stood in her kitchen feeling numb. She couldn't go to the funeral. She had chosen to be with her friend when her friend needed her most. Two months before, she had spent a week in California nursing Leigh and caring for her five-year-old son.

She had fixed meals and put them in the freezer for the weeks to come. She had done laundry, stocked the pantry, cleaned house. Nancy had chosen to spend a week with her friend while her friend was still able to recognize her, still able to remember.

Now it was a week before Easter, and Nancy was supposed to get her family packed and ready to go out of town to be with relatives. Nancy didn't want to pack, didn't want to do Easter egg hunts, didn't want to go out of town. She simply wanted to grieve the death of her friend.

In the hours after learning of Leigh's death, Nancy sat down and wrote a long letter to the hospital chaplain, telling him who Leigh was apart from the disease that took her life. Writing the letter helped; it became the cornerstone of Leigh's eulogy. But Good Friday came early that year for Nancy, and the week before Easter was long and dark.

Easter weekend. Clothes were clean. The car was filled with gas. Everything was packed. The next morning Mark, Nancy, and their two kids would pile in the car, drive eight hours, and spend Easter with Mark's family, a gathering Nancy usually looked forward to. But this Easter was different. This year Nancy resented the coming celebration. She resented the upbeat cheerfulness of Easter bunnies, tulips, and the promise of new life.

As Mark and Nancy were getting ready to leave, the emotions began surfacing. She was no longer numb. First the tears. Then an incredible wave of anger: the reality of Leigh's death, the injustice of brain cancer, the finality of losing a best friend, the tragedy of losing one so young. The anger, grief, resentment, and frustration overpowered the immediate plans to get out the door and on the road.

"I was in our bedroom getting dressed, and I began to feel so angry!" Nancy said. "I was angry at God, angry at Leigh, angry at Mark. I resented having to leave town. Mark was taking a shower and I remember going into the bathroom, throwing open the shower door, and ranting and raving. Mark was scared to death! He stood there while I was going on and on and asked me, 'Nance, are you going to hit me?'

"But you know, that was when I felt closest to God. I realized as painful as that was, if I could be *that* angry at God, then God was really real. I couldn't be that angry at something that *might* be. I found myself wondering, 'How can this be? So painful, but so grateful all at the same time.'

"When Leigh died, I was so mad that God let it happen. But then I knew that God was providing comfort. Even in the dark hour, God was there. God walked through it with me. God is gracious enough to take lousy little fragments left over and turn them into something good.

"Was it [Frederick] Buechner who said, 'All religious experiences begin with a lump in the throat'? When I think about Mark and my kids, when I think about people or experiences that have really touched me, I have a real sense of gratitude. I'd have to say that's when I've felt closest to God."

WHEN DO WE FEEL CLOSEST TO GOD?

Being honest with God in our anger. Watching a child at play. Cooking a meal for a friend. Hearing a voice on the phone. Ordinary moments, but sacramental nonetheless. The moments we feel closest to God are as varied as the women we surveyed.

All religious experiences begin with a lump in the throat. From the mundane to the monumental, women's experiences of faith are as richly varied, as distinctly textured as the tapestries of their lives. Each woman I interviewed—to a person—expressed great surprise and disbelief that I would want to interview *her* for a book on Christian women, considering her own story, experiences, and perspective nothing particularly unique or noteworthy. Yet each woman interviewed, and many of those surveyed, has expressed great curiosity about our findings.

Joanna Bowen Gillespie, in a pioneering book about women's faith experience in four mainline Protestant congregations, wrote, ". . . to date the least studied, least known element in the process of religious change is that involving the female segment of . . . church members in the United States. . . . Men's views of religion have dominated all aspects of the writings and the institutions of religion since the early church banished house churches at the end of the first century. Men's thoughts and structures have been the norm against which all church members have been measured and have evaluated themselves."[1]

When asked, "When do you feel closest to God?" without exception the women I interviewed spoke in simple words, describing poignant moments in everyday lives—and then apologized for their answers being so "untheological" or questioned whether anyone would find anything of value in what they had said.

One woman said she feels closest to God "when I watch my husband reading a bedtime story to my daughters and he doesn't know I'm watching."

Another woman, who has been a visionary, instigator, and proactive advocate of community programs for women and children, sat quietly for a few moments, then pensively said:

> It used to be within the framework of [worship] services at this church, but now it's more when I'm curled up on my window bench at home reading Scripture and thinking, trying to get some instruction.
>
> Somehow the word "calling" has such a high connotation and I just do what I do. I feel that I'm almost pulled into situations and it's other people who tell me it was a "calling." If something bumps up against my ethical base, I have to do something about it! I get into something because I feel so strongly. I don't call it a "calling," but I suppose that's what it is.

This woman has held leadership positions on countless community boards, worked actively in the establishment of crisis nurseries for children at risk, pioneered programs giving gifted children from inner-city neighborhoods exceptional educational opportunities, and organized one-on-one support for families caring for victims of Alzheimer's. She is one of countless "marketplace" missionaries who hear the voice of God and take action. Yet her humility is endearing—and almost comical.

When do women feel closest to God? When a friend dies? While driving children to school or tucking them in at night? In quiet moments alone? The answer is an unequivocal *yes* to each of these moments and countless more. Whether in the darkest of personal crises or moments of profound gratitude, Christian women today experience their relationship with God as a vital lifeline running through the multiple roles, demanding schedules, and challenging realities of their everyday worlds.

Our research reveals that Christian women feel their relationship to God is very important in their lives, more important in fact than church involvement. Yet these are the women who attend church regularly, the women who actively serve in volunteer capacities. These are the women teaching Sunday school, serving on boards and committees, volunteering their time despite limitations on their time.

Why do the women who serve in churches, when asked, respond that God is essential to their lives, yet church involvement is optional? Why do women say that church is where we serve, not where we find spiritual nurturing? Why is church *not* a primary source for spiritual growth for so many of us? Why do so many women, when given an opportunity to say so, respond that they don't feel supported by their churches? Why do women list nearly every other arena of their lives as a place they feel close to God, but rarely mention church?

As Miriam and I wrestled with the survey results, we found these questions particularly disturbing, these findings particularly intriguing. Although we readily admit we are not social scientists nor clinical statisticians, the fact that only 38 percent of the women surveyed feel that women are fairly represented in their local church's decisions—little more than a third—is a startlingly low percentage. Nearly *two-thirds* of the women active in local churches *don't* feel fairly represented. This is cause for concern. The fact that 52 percent believe that the Bible teaches that women can hold leadership positions in churches, yet most churches continue to have predominantly male leadership, is also cause for concern. Joanna Gillespie takes our complacency to task in questions she raises in *Women Speak:*

> More pointedly, what attracts and sustains women in the religious structure that has always been patriarchal, with minimal or totally invisible female participation in leadership or policymaking (until the 1970s)? What do today's women find in an institution that historically equated female passivity and subservience to (male) religious authority with "holiness"? At the time women's "good works" were supplying, almost solely, the funds and volunteers for outreach programs, official male voices in congregations idealized such productive dutifulness as the evidence of spiritual virtue.

Miriam and I have dialogued, e-mailed, written, and queried each other regarding the issues of women, church, and spirituality. We offer the following observations, not for the purpose of naysaying local congregations or the evangelical church at large, but to further dialogue among ourselves as sisters in Christ and, hopefully, to challenge the status quo.

HONEST-TO-GOD CHECKPOINTS FOR TODAY'S CHURCH

- First, although the question of women in leadership in churches may not generate controversial sound bytes in the media today, it continues to be a significant issue in most churches. The question of women in leadership is far from

resolved: passions run high, opinions are polarized, and unfortunately the glass ceiling in churches is much lower than
in the workplace.

- Second, for many women church is clearly not the place we
  feel the closest to God, nor is it a source of support. Women
  value and appreciate their churches; they feel churches are
  conveyors of religious education for their children; many of
  their significant friendships are formed within the context of
  their churches. But personal, vocational, and emotional support for most women is found elsewhere.

- Third, churches claim to be institutions supporting "family
  values," yet it is questionable that they are functioning as
  family-friendly institutions. The gap between family values
  and family-friendly policies seems to be widening in many
  churches.

THE QUESTION OF WOMEN IN LEADERSHIP

Fact: Most women active in community organizations outside the church function in leadership capacities; however, the
same is not true within the church.

Fact: Women surveyed are regularly serving in a ministry in
their church. However, the range of positions in which they serve
does not match the range of gifts listed in Romans 12:6–8.

The survey results show that women gifted in leadership and
administration are most likely to use their gifts *outside* the body
of believers. Sadly, women who *do* serve in leadership positions
are twice as likely to do so *outside* their church, despite the fact
that more than half believe the Bible teaches that women can
hold leadership positions in the church.

Unfortunately, those of us who have strong leadership skills
are often frustrated or restricted in serving our churches. As
we've already said, the glass ceiling is much lower in churches
than in the workplace.

I confess that I was taken by surprise by the impassioned

dialogue among Christian women regarding women in leadership in the church. While preparing to speak to a church group on the findings of this survey, I stumbled into a Christian dialogue forum while "netsurfing" on the cyberspace airways of America Online, a computerized online network service.

In that forum the polarity among women on this issue was at times painfully, at times humorously, apparent. Here are a few of those comments from women with vastly differing viewpoints:

> Nothing like a hot topic! Of course women should be in church leadership. Although I've gotten into a lot of hot water for saying this, in my opinion a church that functions on the basis of male leadership functions with only half the mind of Christ.

> _____

> I've spent a great deal of time thinking about the role of the woman in the church. I know all the arguments. I know times have changed. I know that I am completely capable of a leadership role in the church. Maybe God is okay with women leaders.
>
> But what if He's not? What if it IS a big deal with Him?
>
> I don't know about anybody else, but I'm just not willing to risk crossing God—even if it means giving up an opportunity to serve in a leadership capacity. I've decided to serve Him in other ways, and I think I can learn to accept my role. Anybody else feel this way?

> _____

> I heard Elizabeth Elliot on the radio last week saying that women are the only ones who seem to have trouble understanding the meaning of submissiveness. She said that men understand the idea in terms of military submission . . . that there has to be an authority, etc. But women seem to question these passages of Scripture because we somehow feel it is a negative thing to be submissive. . . . Just be-

cause the husband is to be the head of the family as Christ
is the head of the church, does not mean that women are
subservient or powerless.

Apparently Elizabeth Elliot knows little about the military. The military is a meritocracy, meaning anyone can be
promoted if a person has the merit. The leaders have
worked for their positions due to their skills and experience; therefore women can, and do, ascend to the top
ranks. . . . There's a big difference between a system based
on merit and a system that keeps one group in power at the
permanent expense of another group.

A relationship is either equal or unequal; it can't be half
equal or part equal. If one member has more power, more
authority, more leadership, the other member gets second-
class citizenship.

Let's apply this same dominant/submissive principle to
the races. Let's say whites are determined to be the heads of
society and nonwhites are destined to be the "helpers" or
"supporters" or any other nice term that women are supposed to be content with. And when the nonwhites object
to this lopsided arrangement, you can tell them that just
because they can't be leaders doesn't mean that they aren't
equal. It doesn't mean that they are subservient or powerless.

Of course this arrangement is unthinkable. But if it is
unacceptable to treat an entire race this way, what makes it
acceptable to treat an entire gender this way?

It seems to me that the analogy of white/nonwhite superiority versus male/female superiority has a lot of validity.
I don't know how many times I've been asked to consider
the place of women in the church based only upon the restrictive passages in Scripture. What would happen today if
we based our race relations on the slave/master passages?

Churches, to their everlasting shame, have supported the demeaning institution of slavery by use of inappropriate proof texts. Now, they are doing the same to women. The very sad result is that we give the impression that God is a man. Don't get me wrong. I'm not saying that God is a woman. But God is above and transcends gender, and has mandated that the image of God come from both male and female. Yet in how many church services do we get the impression that God is anything but male?

These are only five of the dialogue entries in the forum; there were several hundred! The issue of women in leadership in the church is not dormant, resolved, or mute. The issue is, at best, being questioned, challenged, and changed; at worst, it is below the surface and festering.

We are told in Romans 12 that needs in the body are met by the use of gifts in the body. Eight gifts listed in Romans 12:6–8 are given to believers. (Paul addresses this passage to *adelphoi*, here meaning everyone in the body—"brothers and sisters." See Romans 12:1, NRSV.) All members of the body of Christ (women as well as men) are given at least one gift. Women surveyed are regularly serving in ministries in their churches. However, the range of positions in which they serve does not match the range of gifts listed in Scripture. Sadly, the obvious conclusion is that churches are not utilizing gifts as God has given them.

God is not in the business of withholding gifts. So why are women restricted from serving in whatever capacity best suits their spiritual gifts? Unused gifts mean unmet needs, a radical loss to the recipient of the gift, the person with the need, and the body of Christ as a whole.

Can the body of Christ afford not to examine their traditional conclusions regarding the use of women's gifts? In the light of increasing changes that challenge our faith and the increasing difficulty of running the race, can we continue traditional practices that allow gifts to lie dormant? Or as one woman asked in the online forum:

> Clearly there is no gender-linking with the gifts as distributed by the Holy Spirit. Clearly as well, Jesus entrusted women with the most important message of all, and seemed to place no restrictions on them. Why, then, are our voices silenced in the church, the place where most of all we are to live out our responsibilities as members of the body of Christ? Is the work of Christ enhanced when half of this body does not have the opportunity to develop fully? Isn't the overriding issue that the world is dying without Christ? I find it extraordinarily sad that so much talent and desire to serve is hampered [by] gender issues.

Leith Anderson, pastor of a large suburban church and author of several books, wrote in an article for *Christianity Today*, "The challenge for the church will be to find meaningful work that fits both women's schedules and giftedness. Already hundreds of churches are using volunteer service directors who serve more as advocates for lay persons than recruiters for Sunday school teachers and other positions."

Miriam and I don't wish to enter the fray of dueling Bible verses and scriptural exegesis. We will leave that for the biblical scholars, feminists, and theologians. We, too, simply find it extraordinarily sad that so much talent and desire to serve is hampered by gender issues.

WHERE WE SEEK A SAFE HAVEN

Women are seldom accused of being "detached" or "distanced" from our emotions. Quite the contrary. The author of the bestselling *Men Are From Mars, Women Are From Venus* has made a truckload of money by striking a resounding chord when he says "men compartmentalize." Women, on the other hand, "integrate." Who we are relationally, vocationally, and spiritually blends and merges. We don't easily compartmentalize one arena from another. Yet the church has too often compartmentalized life experience from spirituality.

An unfortunate dichotomy exists between the message we hear on Sunday mornings and the reality of our lives the rest of the week. And this dichotomy is nothing new.

Nearly a hundred years ago, Charles Reynolds Brown wrote in a study book on Job,

> . . . busy people of the world today . . . commonly find themselves puzzled. They listen to the warm assurances of faith put forth from the pulpits of the land . . . [a God who] does not suffer even a sparrow to fall to the ground without His notice; a Father who is more ready to hear and answer the prayerful appeals of His people than earthly fathers are to give bread to their children; an All-embracing Providence whose affectionate interest in our well-being counts the very hairs on our heads! Then on Monday mornings they go out into the world. . . . They rub against the unplaned side of it and find it rough, full of knots and splinters. They are torn and bruised by the contact. . . . They ponder the apparent discrepancies between the warm theories of the pulpit and the cold facts which face them.

A century later, the dichotomy between warm faith and cold facts continues to be a reality. The "God talk" within evangelical churches is characteristically "victorious," "triumphant," "joyful"—strikingly at odds with Christians' daily experiences of disappointment, injustice, pain, and suffering.

Old Testament scholar Walter Brueggeman addresses this incongruity in an excellent book, *The Message of the Psalms*. Pointing out the fact that nearly one-third of the book of Psalms consists of "laments" which he calls "psalms of disorientation," Brueggeman asserts that these "laments" challenge the assumption that our life of faith is always well ordered, full of blessing, coherence, and equilibrium.

Brueggeman writes of the modern church:

> It is a curious fact that the church has, by and large, continued to sing songs of orientation in a world increasingly experienced as disorientation. That may be laudatory. . . . Such a "mismatch" between our life experience of disorientation and our faith speech of orientation could be a great evangelical "nevertheless". . . .
>
> But at best, this is only partly true. It is my judgment that this action of the church is less an evangelical defiance guided by faith, and much more a numb denial . . . that does not want to acknowledge or experience the disorientation of life. . . . Such a denial . . . is an odd inclination for passionate Bible users, given the large number of psalms that are songs of lament. . . . At least it is clear that a church that goes on singing "happy songs" in the face of raw reality is doing something very different from what the Bible itself does.[2]

As women, we don't compartmentalize. We've known for a long time that what we hear on Sunday and what we experience Monday through Saturday are frequently incongruent. We go to church to serve, to teach our children Christian values, and to participate in worship within the community of faith. But we go elsewhere to heal, to pray, to minister to each other. We go elsewhere when we experience the "disorientation" of marital trouble, teens in crisis, or job loss.

When our lives are living "laments," the victorious "God talk" can be especially painful. One woman who has been a member of her church for more than twenty years confided, hesitantly, that she and her husband were "sorta trying a separation," but they weren't telling many people. She didn't want word to get out in the church. Her church wasn't a place to heal; her church wasn't the place she turned to as a safe haven.

Author Joyce Landorf Heatherly has said, "Real Christians

hold a young woman's hand after she has just miscarried and do not say a word."[3] The evangelical church has much to learn about holding a young woman's hand and not saying a word: not proclaiming victory answers, not offering words of assurance, not singing songs of praise, all to the exclusion of embracing the reality of lament.

The inner-city mothers of children killed as innocent victims of gang violence know the anguish of lament.

The sister of a young woman in jail for violating parole knows the confusion of lament.

The professional woman who walks away from her career when advancement requires compromising her commitment to Christ knows the uncertainty of lament.

The friend of a thirty-three-year-old woman who died from brain cancer the week before Easter knows the reality of lament.

The crucified Jesus cries out in lament on Good Friday, "My God, my God, why have you forsaken me?" And days later, from the empty tomb the question is answered: "He is not here. He is risen."

Although the church undoubtedly has blind spots where women's issues are concerned, Christian women today know where to go to find the safe haven. As we live our commitment to Christ, we live through the lament of Good Friday and seek the empty tomb of Easter. Women were the first to be given the news, "He is not here. He is risen." Cultural limitations, stereotypes, and prescribed roles notwithstanding, we are now—and have always been—messengers of resurrection. Some things never change.

NOTES

1. Joanna Bowen Gillespie, *Women Speak: of God, Congregations and Change.* (Valley Forge, Pa.: Trinity Press International, 1995), pp. 2, 5.
2. Walter Brueggeman, *The Message of the Psalms: A Theological*

Commentary. (Minneapolis: Augsburg Publishing House, 1984), pp. 52–53.

3. Joyce Landorf, *Monday Through Saturday.* (Waco, Tex.: Word Books, 1984), p. 20.

Ten

Monday Through Saturday:
Christian Women Today

Miriam *speaks:*

Several years ago, Kermit the Frog, the emcee of *The Muppet Show*, sang a song called, "It's Not Easy Being Green." The message of the song was that it was hard enough to be a frog—and in addition to that to be green?—well, that was a real problem. Christian women today can relate. It has never been easy to be a woman.

Historically, reading about the lives of women does not make for good bedtime fare. Whether being female during the rise and fall of the Roman Empire, a black female in the United States in 1850, a baby girl in China today, or a sixty-year-old woman in Russia, being a woman extracts a price.

Being a CHRISTIAN woman combines a blessing and a curse in a simple, yet profound way. We have the best of all Saviors from every disadvantage, every injustice, every pain we've ever suffered. We also carry the additional burden of much false theology inflicted in the name of our Creator. At the risk of sounding trite, *It's not easy being green.*

While Christians in our Western culture may decry the false theology of cults that consider women chattel—veiled and voiceless—in too many evangelical, fundamental churches and parachurch organizations, Christian women are still veiled and voiceless, "seen" but not heard.

But I do not despair my lot as a Christian woman today. While knowing from my walk, one day at a time, that God is real and good, hundreds of women share positive faith.

My survey reveals good news of what Christian women are *not*:

1. We are not "missionless" in God's kingdom.

2. We are not hiding our talents that are rejected by the church.

3. We are not wilting in our zeal to love our Creator and bring glory to Him.

My survey reveals good news of what Christian women *are*:

1. Our mission place has moved to the marketplace.

2. Our needy culture accepts and utilizes our gifts to help our communities. (Our testimony will follow.)

3. We treasure our Creator, and our resulting spiritual walk is incredibly important to us.

While my survey documents this for 1,000 Christian women, my experiences in a recent eight-week time period also highlight good news about Christian women today. I have had the opportunity to (1) visit Russia to distribute literature in train stations and marketplaces, as well as worship in local churches, (2) attend a conference on the theological underpinnings of the equality of all believers, including studying the original texts, and (3) attend a conference of Christian booksellers interacting with the movers of Christian literature in one segment of our Christian culture and extensively interview authors of books and music. My observations during these eight weeks include this good news about Christian women:

- They are leading people to Jesus, young and old, male and female; introducing them to their Savior on street corners, in churches, on airplanes; praying the new believer's prayer with children, middle-agers, and elders.
- They are studying the Word of God, excellent students of the original languages, translating the texts minus the masculine filter that has predominated for centuries.
- They are networking the Word to hungry believers, willing to teach against the tide. They are broadcasting from heart to heart, fingertip to fingertip, their love and commitment to the One who is the Word.
- They are willing believers, willing to fast, pray, write, sing, whatever they are called to do. One closed channel is not the last word to Christian women today. Closed doors are a challenge to today's Christian women. Closed channels simply intensify their efforts and creativity to serve their Maker.

The river of God's love cannot be dammed to be hoarded by a select few. The Great Commission cannot be silenced for half of God's grateful converts bursting with the message that Jesus will bring new life to any tired, misused, messed-up human being.

WHAT MOTIVATES TODAY'S CHRISTIAN WOMEN?

What has impacted today's Christian women? What threads have woven this tapestry, created this welcome mat, provided the motive behind the momentum of today's Christian women? (Not listed in order of significance.)

- *Technology.* The printing press gave the Word to anyone who could read. Telephones, fax machines, computers, e-mail, microphones, satellites, enable us to communicate with others our thoughts, dialogue, questions.
- *Equality.* Yes, the early feminists, such as Susan B. Anthony,

empower Christian women today. In fact, many early feminists were Christians. This should come as no surprise. Jesus
was radical in His conversations with women and His instructions to them. Feminist pressure in past decades has
moved women into educational institutions, increased wom-
en's literacy, increased women's voice in the dialogue of humans.

Unfortunately, the word "feminist" has come to mean
"anti-Christian" because voices that contradict the Word
have drowned out Christian women in what is now called
the "feminist movement." However, the original, pure sense
of equality has ushered women out of dependence on knowing a god described to them by another human, into a direct
relationship with God, open Bible on our laps.

What woman, or man for that matter, can look directly
into Jesus' eyes full of compassion, forgiveness, fairness,
power, pleasure, pure love with no hidden agenda, and not
lay out her being to partner with Him wherever He leads?
Equality positions us to look at Him directly.

- *Hope.* I recently wandered up a side street in Tula, Russia. I
could not help but notice an old woman struggling up the
street from the train station toward apartments on a hillside.
She stopped, put down her bucket, sat on some concrete
steps, and put her head on her knees. I paused, thinking she
might tumble over and need my assistance. But she did not.
She rose again, mouth set in a firm line midst wrinkles criss-
crossing wrinkles on her placid face. She put one rubber boot
in front of the other and hauled her load on up the broken
sidewalk, head tilted up as if in an effort to reach for more
breath.

She stopped and sagged slightly toward nothing, and
then straightened herself. One boot in front of another, one
boot in front of another. Passersby ignored her, maybe accustomed to such a sight. To be an old woman in Russia to-

day is not a blessed life-style. She did not acknowledge my presence, nor I hers, though we were both aware. It was as if she were drawn to a destiny in some small apartment ahead: waiting for a government check that might never come, breathing in air that her tired body could not absorb. No reason to smile.

The next day dawned new and fresh with a vivid contrast. A young girl, possibly twelve, greeted me cheerfully. "Good morning." Energetic blue eyes looked directly into mine. "Good morning, what is your name?" I responded and quickly discovered she had used her entire English vocabulary. We understood mutual smiles; that was all. I gave her literature. Moments later I saw her perched on the edge of a step, avidly reading the book I had given her, *More Than a Carpenter.*

She returned to me smiling. While more attempts at conversation proved futile, we felt like friends. She shadowed me and communicated that she wanted to help pass out our books. I don't know how much she read of *More Than a Carpenter* sitting on that step. I do know that she was a persuasive distributor of books, answering questions in a language I did not know, convincing those who hesitated, radiantly on a mission. She worked with our group for over an hour. She seemed a bit distraught to have to leave us but waved as she caught her bus. The look on her face was worlds apart from the old woman. Same town, same week, same gender. Different expectation for the future: *hope.*

WHAT DOES THE FUTURE HOLD FOR CHRISTIAN WOMEN?

Some feel the answer rests significantly on what the role of Christian women will be in the body of believers, the church. Will women be welcomed in the pulpits of American churches? While the answer to that question may be significant to the health and ministry potential of American churches, I believe it is insignificant to God's fulfilling His Great Commission through women. As I said earlier, the love of God cannot be dammed to be enjoyed by a select few.

He will reach others through us.

While the churches of America have been great facilitators in broadcasting God's message to our country in the past, that era may be over. Indeed, few would disagree that many mainline churches are dwindling, and the lukewarm factor has permeated many Christians so that we resemble an army with the momentum of molasses on a cold day. But that is us in our culture, not God in us in our world.

The significant question remains, is the Great Commission still of utmost importance to God? Unequivocally, the answer is, "Yes!" Then each of us must answer, "What am I doing in light of that great directive from my Creator?"

May you be encouraged to know that women are going into the marketplace as though it is their mission field. Pulpit is replaced by priority mailroom, altar is replaced by any space women can pray—with eyes open, focused on a computer screen, or focused on a co-worker who needs the truth of who made him or her. We have the high privilege of introducing anyone and everyone to Jesus.

When Jesus rode into Jerusalem, His followers and even children cheered Him and announced who He was. Some, with less than noble intent, remarked that these ragtag heralders should be silenced. Jesus' answer: "If they were silent the very stones would cry out." Jesus WILL be introduced; He will be announced. The question is not whether, but by whom.

Who shall announce Him? We shall—today's Christian women. Jesus commissioned all believers. His love for us compels us; our love for Him lifts us high above an "it's not easy being green" attitude. We're on a mission. If not visible, our actions will begin ripples of faith. If not heard, our expressions of love will be felt from prison cells to school halls, to factory floors, to homes, and hospitals, and presidents' boardrooms.

Who are Christian women today?

We are not gender-bound people. We are Christians!

Section Four

References and Resources

Appendix A
The Neff Report: Christian Women in Today's Church and Society

The following questions were designed by a Christian woman, counselor, and author to find out what other Christian women think about the role of women in the church, society, and home.

Statistical analysis was completed on 1,052 surveys out of the 1,200 returned. This includes surveys taken in church groups and Christian organizations from different geographic locations, ranging from New York to California.

POPULATION

Race

White	63%
Black	24%
Hispanic	4%

Asian   2%
Other   1%

Employment

Which of the following best describes your present employment status and, if married, that of your spouse?

	Self	**Spouse**
Employed F/T 30+ hrs	61%	47%
Employed P/T -30 hrs	12%	2%
Homemaker	15%	
Retired	15%	6%
Temporarily unemployed	7%	4%
Attending school	6%	2%

If employed outside the home, what type of occupation do you have?

Office worker	20%
Medical professional	10%
Education	9%
Management	9%
Sales	5%
Technical	4%
Medical technical	3%
Church staff	2%
Skilled trade	1%
Legal professional	1%
Legal technical	1%

CHECK/NOTE

- While the majority (50%) are content with their primary vocation, 4 in 10 (40%) would like further training—not necessarily a degree.

- 3 in 10 (29%) wish to acquire a higher degree.
- Only 1 in 10 (12%) agree that they received adequate educational counseling.

Current marital status

Married	51%
Single	18%
Divorced, not remarried	14%
Divorced and remarried	6%
Widowed	4%
Separated	3%
Widowed and remarried	1%
Total "been married at one time"	82%
Total "currently married"	58%
Total "currently single"	36%

CHECK/NOTE

- Black women: Married 35%; single never married 30%; divorced 20%; and separated 6%.

Income

Single median $27,000
Married $53,000 (combined income)
No degree median $35,000
Degreed $44,000

Children

Yes	70%
No	30%

Average number of children living at home is 2.1.

CHECK/NOTE

- 2 in 3 whites (66%) have no children at home compared with 2 in 10 blacks (20%); 1 in 4 others (25%).

Education
What is the highest level of education?

High school graduate   95%
Some college   63%

CHECK/NOTE

- The overwhelming majority of respondents (95%) are high school graduates. 1 in 2 (50%) has a college degree or higher.
- Single women are significantly more likely to be employed than married women (85% vs. 64%). Black women are more likely to be employed than white women (81% vs. 68%).
- Top positions for degreed women:

Education	14%
Medical programs	14%
Office work	13%
Management	11%

- Top position for non-degreed women is office work (20%).
- Degreed women are more diversified in position than non-degreed.
- Those who attended a Christian institution of learning most likely attended a Christian college.

Median age
40.58

Location of home
Suburban   54%
Urban   22%

Small town (non-metropolitan)   9%
Rural   7%

ABOUT YOURSELF

Stress

The following stresses are currently present in your life (percent who have this stress):

Job-related stress	38%
Inadequate financial income	34%
Parenting responsibilities	31%
Physical health	22%
Marital difficulties	17%
Difficult relationship other than spouse or child(ren)	17%
Taking care of older parents	14%
Under-employment	8%
Possible unemployment	7%
Unemployment	4%
Physical safety	4%

CHECK/NOTE

- 4 in 10 singles currently have financial stress in their lives compared to 3 in 10 marrieds.
- Singles are significantly more likely to experience job-related stress (48% compared to marrieds 33%).
- Nearly half of black women (46%) are experiencing financial stress compared to whites (30%); other races (36%).
- Black women are more likely to have a single income and hold lower-paying jobs.
- Other races (29%) are significantly more likely than whites (18%) or blacks (12%) to cite marital difficulties as a current stress.

- White women (26%) are significantly more stressed about their physical health than black women (14%).
- White women (18%) are significantly more stressed than black women (6%) regarding taking care of parents.

I feel positive about myself because:

I can feel God's love	85%
I am serving others	8%
My family experience is satisfying	53%
My work is worthwhile	10%
I am self-sufficient	11%
I like the way I look	52%
Other	9%

I don't feel positive about myself because:

My family experience is not satisfying	21%
I can't feel God's love	6%
I don't like the way I look	22%
I am not serving others	8%
My work is not worthwhile	10%
I am not self-sufficient	11%
Other	9%

CHECK/NOTE

- Singles (61%) are significantly more positive about self because they are self-sufficient compared to marrieds (40%).
- Marrieds (54%) feel more positive about self because of their satisfying family experience compared to singles (38%). (I thought family experience for marrieds would be stronger.)

If you work outside the home, what are the rewards of your choice?

The MOST rewarding:
Fulfilling my spiritual calling   48%

Financial benefits	46%
Personal need for a sense of identity/ self	20%
Primary benefit is to others in the family	18%
Using my skills and abilities	17%
A career	10%
Medical benefits	9%
Interaction with others	9%

Options that you AGREE with:

I am content with my primary vocation	50%
I would like further training, not necessarily a degree	40%
I wish to acquire a higher degree	29%
I received adequate educational counseling	12%
I have achieved a higher degree than I need or use	9%

CHECK/NOTE
Rewards:

- Majority: fulfilling my spiritual calling.
- Single women: financial benefit of working outside the home.
- Black and other races: significant medical benefits.
- Whites: significant personal need for sense of identity.
- Over half of married women are content with primary vocation (55% vs. singles 42%).
- Women without degree evenly divided between content with primary vocation and wanting more training (46%/46%).
- Degreed women (55%) are content with their primary vocations.

Family

If you are married, who does each of the following tasks in your home?

	Doesn't apply	Mainly wife	Shared equally	Mainly husband
Cooks meals	6	73	17	4
Does the housework	9	71	18	2
Does grocery shopping	5	67	21	7
Does the dishes	7	59	26	7
Does the vacuuming	11	58	18	13
Balances checkbook	7	53	15	25
Arranges/plans social activities	8	49	41	2
Leads/initiates devotions/ Bible study	17	44	30	9
Takes out garbage	9	21	27	44
Makes major family home decisions	6	11	73	13
Does yardwork	20	10	19	51
Looks after/maintains car(s)	9	8	20	63

CHECK/NOTE

- In other races (70%), black (74%), it is significantly more likely that the wife mainly balances checkbook (whites, 56%).
- In black marriages it is significantly more likely that doing dishes is shared than in white marriages.
- In other races mates are more likely to share equally in housework than whites.
- Who leads/initiates devotions/Bible study? Blacks: 59% wife leads; other races: 52% wife leads; white: 43% wife leads.
- Majority (78%) make major family/home decisions together. Of those where not equally shared, black wives are signifi-

cantly more likely to make major family decisions than white wives.

For those who do or did have children at home, the following tasks are/were done by:

	Mainly wife	Shared equally	Mainly husband
Coordinates children's schedule	90	9	1
Manages children's needs	88	11	1
Cares for the children	80	19	1
Changes diapers	70	29	1
Gives attention to their spiritual growth/development	61	38	1
Listens to their problems when they're hurting	58	41	1
Administers discipline	54	49	5
Plays with the children	35	59	6

CHECK/NOTE

- The majority of women are married (58%) and do the majority of the housework except for: maintaining the automobile (63% husband), yardwork (51% husband), and taking out the garbage, which they share—49% of wives either mainly take it out or equally share it with their husbands.
- Vast majority of wives coordinate children's schedules.

About Your Experiences

Using a scale from 1 to 5 where 1 is "safety" and 5 is "abuse," respondents described their sexual, physical, and emotional childhood as:

	Mean	%
Abused	—	—
Sexually safe	1.17	15%

Physically safe	1.18	12%
Emotionally safe	1.76	30%

If abused, individuals involved

Sexual	other relative 38%, other 34%, father 25%, sister/brother 18%, mother 5%
Physical	father 48%, sister/brother 14%, other relative 11%, other 11%, mother 4%
Emotional	mother 65%, father 61%, sister/brother 11%, other relative 8%, other 6%

For those who experienced any abuse, the following best describes your church's role in helping you heal from these past traumas:

Action of church	Percentage who experienced it
Is/was unaware	57%
Helped me heal	32%
Was aware but did not address hurts	6%
Made me feel guilty	4%
Was aware, tried to help, made me feel worse	2%

7 in 10 (71%) of respondents chose to describe their first sexual experience. They described it as follows:

Desired equally by the other person and me	51%
Desired more by other person than me	35%
Not desired by me	12%
Desired more by me than other person	3%

7 in 20 (35%) admitted that after the age of 21, they feel they did something sexually inappropriate with someone other than their spouse.

Yes	35%
No	42%
No response	23%

Of those 7 in 20 (35%) who admitted to doing something sexually inappropriate after age 21 with someone other than their spouse, 1 in 3 (32% or 13% of total) were married at the time.

1 in 3 (33%) respondents admitted to having sexual intercourse after age 21 with someone other than their spouse.

Yes	32%
No	37%
No response	30%

Of those who have had sexual intercourse after age 21 with someone other than their spouse, 1 in 3 (35% or 12 % of total) were married at the time.

Have you ever had an abortion?

Yes	18%
No	64%
No response	18%

If yes, what was the reason?

Medical necessity	9%
Pregnancy was the result of incest/rape	5%
Pregnancy not wanted by me	86%

Are you satisfied with your present sexual life?

Yes, very satisfied	18%
Yes, satisfied	13%

Yes, it is nonexistent	13%
Somewhat satisfied	12%
No, mildly dissatisfied	5%
No, very dissatisfied	4%
No, it is nonexistent	15%
No response	20%

CHECK/NOTE

- White women (42%) were much more likely to describe their first sexual experience as equally desired by themselves.
- Black women (36%) were much more likely to describe their first sexual experience as desired more by the other than by themselves. Whites (22%); others (25%).
- Since age 21, have you ever done anything with someone (not spouse) that you feel was sexually inappropriate? Singles 43%; marrieds 31%.
- Since age 21, have you ever had sexual intercourse with someone other than your spouse? Singles 35%; marrieds 32%.
- Have you had an abortion? 3 in 10, blacks (32%); 1 in 10, whites (12%).
- Regarding being satisfied with your present sexual life, of singles who said it is nonexistent, 38% were satisfied and 37% were not satisfied.
- Nearly 1 in 2 marrieds (48%) is satisfied.

TYPES OF LEADERSHIP POSITIONS IN CHURCH/DENOMINATION WHICH WOMEN MAY HOLD
Position and percentage of women allowed to hold:

Music/choir director	72%
Ministry leader	71%
Sunday school superintendent	66%

Committee/commission leader	65%
Youth director	62%
Adult Sunday school w/men in class	55%
Deacon/deaconess	51%
Chairperson of church board	43%
Trustee	38%
Assistant/associate pastor	35%
Pastor/minister	29%
Elder	27%

Position and percentage of women who have held position in last 12 months:

Ministry leader	46%
Music/choir director	43%
Committee/commission leader	39%
Sunday school superintendent	38%
Adult Sunday school w/men in class	34%
Deacon/deaconess	30%
Youth director	30%
Assistant/associate pastor	18%
Chairperson of church board	17%
Trustee	16%
Elder	13%
Pastor/minister	10%

CHECK/NOTE

- The majority of respondents (51% or greater) indicated that women were allowed to hold the following positions: music/choir director, ministry leader, Sunday school superintendent, committee/commission leader, youth director, adult Sunday school teacher of a class with men in it, and deacon/deaconess.
- However, within the last 12 months, less than one-half of the

respondents have had a woman fill those positions either in their church or denomination.

- The overwhelming majority of women (97%) responded that their current relationship with God is "very important to me now."
- 9 in 10 (89%) stated that "My current church attendance is very important to me now."
- Of the 7 in 10 respondents (72%) who "have been unable to fully utilize their gifts in their local church," 43% cited lack of time; 57% were available.

Statement and percentage who strongly agree:

Men and women are equally helped by my local church (58%).
I believe the Bible teaches that women can hold leadership positions in the church (52%).
Women are fairly represented in my local church's decisions (38%).
I have been able to fully utilize my gifts and talents in my local church (29%).
I believe the Bible teaches that women can be pastors (20%).
Evangelical churches clearly understand what the Bible teaches about women's roles in the church (15%).
I have been able to utilize my gifts and talents outside my local church more than within it (15%).

My values match those of my church on:

Women's roles in families	81%
Women and employment	67%
Women's roles in the church	60%
Reproductive choices	59%
Women's roles in government	49%

If a woman has leadership ability, my church would encourage:

Leading women's ministries	81%
Leading children's ministries	79%
Leadership in missions	67%
Supervising a Sunday school including adults	61%
Leading an adult ministry (including men)	52%
Board membership	44%

If a woman were able to preach, my church would encourage:

Teaching women and/or children	67%
Mission preaching	46%
Preaching in the main service	32%
Full-time preaching	26%

If a woman were able to explain/teach Scripture to men and women, my church would encourage:

Teaching women and/or children	71%
Encourage teaching any class	59%
Encourage teaching in missions	56%
Encourage preaching to the congregation	30%

CHECK/NOTE

- The overwhelming majority of Christian women surveyed (88%) attend church at least once a week (51% twice/wk, and 37% once/wk).
  7 in 10 (70%) of these women serve regularly in a ministry.
  6 in 10 (59%) serve regularly in a ministry in their churches.
  1 in 10 (11%) serves regularly in a ministry in the community.
- Just under one half (44%) of the women who responded regularly serve in a leadership capacity.
- 1 in 3 (35%) exercises leadership in the church—only 6 in

10 of those who serve regularly in a ministry in the church are in a leadership capacity.
- 1 in 10 (9%) exercises leadership in the community—nearly all who serve regularly in a ministry in the community are in a leadership capacity.
- Church involvement has increased for 1 in 2 (50%) of the women over the past 12 months.
- 2 in 3 (66%) think their church involvement will increase in the future.
- Married women are much more likely to state that their church does not offer training for marital satisfaction and preparation to be self-supporting.

SPIRITUAL NEEDS AND RELATIONSHIP TO CHURCH

Rank in order (with 1 being greatest) the support you've received from the church/percentage most helped:

Spiritual inspiration	47%
Spiritual information	43%
Significant relationships with other believers	12%
Training for family living	7%
Training for marital satisfaction	6%
Discovering your talents and gifts	6%
Preparation to be self-supporting	3%
Training for parenting	2%

In what areas of need has the church not given you the help you desired:

Spiritual information	4%
Spiritual inspiration	7%
Training for family living	16%
Training for marital satisfaction	20%
Training for parenting	21%

Discovering your talents and gifts   23%
Preparation to be self-supporting   34%
Significant relationships with other believers 12%

CHECK/NOTE

- Black women are much more likely to attend church twice per week than white women.
- Race is more a factor in frequent church attendance than marital status or education.
- If you are currently married and white, you are significantly more likely to be involved in a leadership capacity at church than if you are single and/or black or of another race.
  (36% married vs. 26% single)
  (38% white vs. 24% black or other)
- The overwhelming majority of black (85%) and other races (70%) think their church involvement will increase in the future.
- Black women's churches are significantly more likely to allow women to hold position of pastor/minister than white women's churches (43% black vs. 25% white).
- One-half of white women's churches (49%) do not allow women to hold position of pastor/minister.
- 1 in 2 black churches (53%) allows women to be assistant/ associate pastor compared to 3 in 10 (29%) white churches.
- Nearly half of white churches do not allow women to be assistant/associate pastors.
- 1 in 4 white women (23%) compared to 1 in 10 black (8%) and other races (10%) is not allowed to be chairperson of church board.
- White women are significantly more likely not to be allowed position as chairperson of church board than black or other.
- Married women (35%) are significantly more likely than sin-

gle women (27%) to be in churches where women are not allowed to be elders.

- White women (41%) are significantly more likely than blacks (15%) or others (14%) to be in churches where women are not allowed to be elders.
- Black women's churches (59%) are significantly more likely than whites (49%) to allow women to be deacons/deaconesses.
- White women's churches (19%) are significantly more likely than black (7%) or other (7%) not to allow women to be deacons.
- White women's churches (16%) are more likely than black or others not to allow them to be trustees or youth directors.
- Nearly 2 in 3 black women's churches (63%) allow women to teach adult Sunday school with men in it compared to approximately 1 in 2 white or other.
- White women's churches are significantly more likely not to allow women to teach adult Sunday school with men in the class than the churches of black or other women.
- Whites (45%) and others (52%) cite lack of time as a more significant reason than blacks for not fully utilizing their gifts in church.
- For married women (47%) lack of time is a more significant reason for not utilizing their gifts in church than for singles (38%).
- Black women (32%) and other races (29%) are significantly more likely than white women (14%) to strongly agree that the Bible teaches that women can be pastors.
- Black women (61%) and other races are significantly more likely than white women (47%) to strongly agree that the Bible teaches that women can hold leadership positions.
- Nearly half of black women (46%) strongly agree that women are fairly represented in their local churches' deci-

sions compared to white women (1 in 3 [35%] strongly agree).

- Women without a college degree (11%) are significantly more likely than those with college degree (5%) to strongly disagree with the statement "I have been able to fully utilize my gifts and talents in my local church."

Appendix B
Recommended
Resources

The following resources are a listing of books that have been either theologically formative or personally meaningful to Miriam Neff and Debra Klingsporn. This listing of resources is not exhaustive, nor is it intended to be a listing of "books every Christian woman should read." *Shattering Our Assumptions* was written to break a few of the cookie-cutter expectations for Christian women—we're not offering a "cookie cutter" listing that is right for every woman. Some of these titles you may find intriguing; some will be of no interest. We offer this listing for you to pick and choose—and we hope these resources will enable you to continue to widen your horizons, expand your understanding of God, and deepen your relationship with the Risen Christ.

Arthur, Kay, Jill Briscoe, Carol Mayhall. *Can A Busy Christian Develop Her Spiritual Life?* Minneapolis: Bethany House Publishers, 1994. Honest and challenging answers about the place of spirituality in women's lives. Written by women for women.

Ashcroft, Mary Ellen. *Temptations Women Face*. Downers Grove, Ill.: InterVarsity Press, 1991. A book about the needs and motivations of women, what temptations hook into those needs, and how women can get beyond them. Addresses envy, anger, our focus on food and dieting, distortions about sex, and others.

Barton, R. Ruth. *Becoming a Woman of Strength.* Wheaton: Harold Shaw Publishers, 1994. An egalitarian approach to what the Scripture says about fourteen areas of stress and challenge for women today, including women in society, marriage, church, careers, and more.

Blue, Ron. *Master Your Money Workbook.* Nashville: Thomas Nelson Publishers, 1993. An easy-to-follow 10-week program using a framework that is biblical and relevant for individuals or couples interested in improving their financial management skills. Includes how to effectively budget, methods for debt reduction, and guidance for long-term investment decisions. The program in this workbook provides the tools and techniques needed to bring order to finances and peace of mind in daily living.

Bondi, Roberta. *Memories of God: Theological Reflections of a Life.* Nashville: Abingdon Press, 1995. Written by a professor of church history at Chandler School of Theology, Emory University, in Atlanta, this book speaks with great simplicity of the particularities of growing up female in middle-class mid-century America, combining profound theological insight with vivid and poignant personal recollection.

Brooke, Avery. *Finding God in the World: Reflections on a Spiritual Journey.* San Francisco: Harper & Row, Publishers, 1989. An intensely personal account of one woman's pilgrimage of faith. Written in the tradition of classic spiritual autobiography, she narrates the experience of her agnostic childhood through to her conversion and eventual role as a spiritual director. A profoundly influential book for DK.

Buechner, Frederick. *Wishful Thinking: A Theological ABC.* New York: Harper & Row, Publishers, 1973. A book DK has pulled off the shelf more often than probably any other, this book is a sometimes whimsical, often enlightening theological dictionary for the restless believer, the doubter, or anyone who wants to redefine or reclaim words that have become an integral part of our daily language.

Evans, Mary J. *Women in the Bible*. Downers Grove, Ill.: InterVarsity Press, 1983. Incorporating careful and thorough evangelical scholarship, this resource surveys all the relevant texts in the Old and New Testaments related to women's roles. Also provides helpful information on cultural and religious influences affecting the New Testament church. An invaluable resource for any woman interested in what biblical scholarship has to say about women's issues.

Gadeberg, Jeanette. *Raising Strong Daughters*. Minneapolis: Fairview Press, 1995. Although not written from an evangelical Christian perspective, this book is nonetheless an invaluable resource for women. Jeanette Gadeberg provides a variety of creative ideas to teach girls of any age the inner confidence, strength, and know-how needed to get ready for life.

Hagberg, Janet O., and Robert A. Guelich. *The Critical Journey: Stages in the Life of Faith*. Salem, Wis.: Sheffield Publishing, 1995, original copyright 1989. An excellent guide for those wrestling with their faith and wondering how others have resolved their "dark nights of the soul." This book describes six phases of the spiritual life and illustrates how people act and think while in each of these stages. Provides compassionate understanding for those who have wondered why everyone doesn't respond in the same manner to the message of the Gospel.

Hayden, Ruth. *How to Turn Your Money Life Around: The Money Book for Women*. Deerfield Beach, Fla.: Health Communications, Inc., 1992. A book written specifically for women, the author brings a deep understanding of the difficulties women face regarding money. Helps women identify attitudes of fear and shame about money, develop useful self-

management skills, and learn how to change their money behavior.

Holt, Patricia. *Ten Myths That Damage a Woman's Confidence.*
Minneapolis: Bethany House Publishers, 1995. Attacks the
myths that keep women from experiencing their rightful
confidence as women of God—a confidence that comes
from faith and God's ability to work in our lives.

Jackson, Donna. *How to Make the World a Better Place for
Women in Five Minutes a Day.* New York: Hyperion, 1992. A
handbook that provides facts, information, and contacts regarding issues that affect women every day. Although the political positions this author advocates on some issues are not
what MN and DK would support, the information she provides on issues from breast cancer research and other medical issues for women to the prevention of teen pregnancy,
to domestic abuse and violence against women are worth the
price of the book.

Keener, Craig S. *The IVP Bible Background Commentary.* Downers Grove, Ill.: InterVarsity Press, 1993. Written in clear,
nontechnical terms, this Bible study aid provides in verse-
by-verse format the crucial cultural background for responsible Bible study as well as a glossary of cultural terms and
important historical figures, an up-to-date bibliography of
commentaries and other resources for each book of the New
Testament, and more.

Louden, Jennifer. *The Woman's Comfort Book: A Self-Nurturing
Guide for Restoring Balance in Your Life.* San Francisco:
HarperSanFrancisco, a division of HarperCollins Publishers,
1992. Although not written from an evangelical Christian
perspective, this is a wonderfully comprehensive resource
for refreshing and replenishing the self. Nurturing comes
naturally to most women—as long as it's directed at someone else. But taking care of yourself is more difficult. For
women too busy to worry about their well-being, this book

includes more than two hundred soothing means of relaxation, self-care, and gentle growth.

Lindbergh, Anne Morrow. *Gift From the Sea*. New York: Pantheon Books, 1975, original copyright 1955. A classic. Eight compelling, unforgettable meditations on youth and age, love and marriage, solitude, peace, and contentment from a woman who was ahead of her time. Beautifully written, graciously timeless. Every Christian woman owes it to herself to savor this one.

Neff, Miriam. *Devotions for Women in the Marketplace*. Chicago: Moody Press, 1991. Based on passages from Proverbs, this book of meditations offers wisdom for making decisions, perspective for setting priorities, and peace for daily living.

Neff, Miriam. *Sisters of the Heart*. Nashville: Thomas Nelson Publishers, 1995. An engaging book of vignettes and sisters' stories of encouragement for women of all ages.

Newenhuyse, Elizabeth Cody. *God, I Know You're Here Somewhere*. Minneapolis: Bethany House Publishers, 1996. Sorts through the craziness and confusion of today's hectic lifestyles and helps women examine their choices and find inner calm amidst a fast-paced schedule.

Schaef, Anne Wilson. *Meditations for Women Who Do Too Much*. San Francisco: Harper & Row, Publishers, 1990. A pocket-sized book of 365 concise meditations for women who find themselves too often over-extended. Combines wisdom, wit, and humor with quotations from women of different ages, cultures, and perspectives.

Sherman, Doug, and William Hendricks. *Your Work Matters to God*. Colorado Springs: Navpress, 1987. For women getting a handle on what God thinks of work and career as it relates to living as people of God, this book is an excellent foundational work. Biblically based, the authors move from texts in Genesis throughout the Scriptures, demonstrating that work isn't an afterthought, but an integral part of God's intentions for us.

Tucker, Ruth A. *Women in the Maze.* Downers Grove, Ill.: InterVarsity Press, 1992. Brief, practical, and responsible answers to dozens of questions Christians ask regarding women and some of the most important controversies facing today's church.

VanVonderen, Jeff. *Families Where Grace Is in Place: Getting Free from the Burden of Pressuring, Controlling, and Manipulating Your Spouse and Children.* Minneapolis: Bethany House Publishers, 1992. A refreshingly honest message about how God's grace can transform relationships within a marriage and family. Despite our desire to "do things right," if we end up tired, discouraged, and feeling like failures, this book is a place to start.

VanVonderen, Jeff. *Tired of Trying to Measure Up.* Minneapolis: Bethany House Publishers, 1989. Written to point the way to freedom for Christians who live under an unwritten religious code of expectations and rules that shame them and drain them of spiritual strength.

Vine, W. E. *The Expanded Vine's Expository Dictionary of New Testament Words.* John R. Kohlenberger III, Editor, Minneapolis: Bethany House Publishers, 1984. Vine's work, a standard reference book since its first publication in 1940, has been the only Greek dictionary for those who do not know Greek. A unique combination of dictionary, concordance, and commentary in one volume, the expanded edition is both more accurate and extensive. An invaluable reference work for every student of the Bible.

Whelchel, Mary. *If You Only Knew.* Wheaton: Victor Books, 1996. Stories of both biblical and contemporary women bring you face-to-face with the life-changing power of God's grace, demonstrating how God transforms ordinary women in the past and continues to do so today.

Whelchel, Mary. *The Christian Working Woman*. Grand Rapids: Fleming H. Revell, a division of Baker Book House, 1994. A successful executive and single mother teaches how to effectively apply Christian commitment to the workplace. Deals with stress, attitudes toward ambition and money, surviving as a working mother, handling job hunting and unemployment, responses to sexual harassment, and more.

Wiederkehr, Macrina. *Seasons of Your Heart*. San Francisco: HarperSanFrancisco, a division of HarperCollins Publishers, 1985. An eloquent and lyrical invitation to journey through the spiritual seasons of wonder, hope, love, mystery, and faith.